To Uncle Steve,
My first published work Tmayo

See pg 16

Oi Rhyme upon a

The West Midlands
Edited by Claire Tupholme

First published in Great Britain in 2011 by:

Young**Writers**

Young Writers
Remus House
Coltsfoot Drive
Peterborough
PE2 9BF
Telephone: 01733 890066
Website: www.youngwriters.co.uk

All Rights Reserved
Book Design by Tim Christian
© Copyright Contributors 2011
SB ISBN 978-0-85739-477-4

THIS BOOK BELONGS TO

....

Foreword

Here at Young Writers our objective is to help children discover the joys of poetry and creative writing. Few things are more encouraging for the aspiring writer than seeing their own work in print. We are proud that our anthologies are able to give young authors this unique sense of confidence and pride in their abilities.

Once Upon A Rhyme is our latest fantastic competition, specifically designed to encourage the writing skills of primary school children through the medium of poetry. From the high quality of entries received, it is clear that Once Upon A Rhyme really captured the imagination of all involved.

The resulting collection is an excellent showcase for the poetic talents of the younger generation and we are sure you will be charmed and inspired by it, both now and in the future.

Contents

Maddie Stewart is our featured poet this year. She has written a nonsense workshop for you and included some of her great poems. You can find these at the end of your book.

Blackheath Primary School, Rowley Regis
Brad Willetts (11) 1
Amy Longden (10) 1
Rachael Bradley (10) 2
Chloe Millward (11) 2
Shannon Kelly (10) 3
Gemma Mittoo (10) 3
Kia Green (10) 4
Jack Bain (10) 4
Brandan Sabin (10) 5
Samuel Hingley (10) 5
Jessica Whitehouse (11) 6
Samuel Robson (10) 6
Charlotte Ockold (11) 7
Jesse Sherwood (10) 7
Alisha Subherwal (10) 8
Chloe Nock (10) 8
Jack James (10) 9
Jack William Powell (11) 9
Drew Forrest (11) 9
Hannah Jordan (10) 10

Brownhills West Primary School, Walsall
Callum Roadknight (8) 10
Anais Morris (7) 10
Jack Cockayne (8) 11
Tanya Griffin (8) 11
Angel Steane (7) 11
Jessica Steane (8) 12

Joe Hipwell (8) 12

Chad Vale Primary School, Edgbaston
Sunny Coco Marko Bennett (8) 12
Amina Mekic (9) 13

Cheslyn Hay Primary School, Walsall
Leon Thomas (8) 13
Paige Stanyard (10) 14
Georgia Barber (11) 15
Olivia Woolley (8) 15
Tomas Ethan Mayo (8) 16
Ellison Yates (8) 16
Elle Mae Phillips (7) 17
James Hickson-Akehurst (8) 17
Morgan Owen (9) 18
Jamie Haldron (9) 18
Sinali Gunarathne (9) 19
Amy-Jo Bickley (10) 19
Joshua Harrison (10) 20
Matthew Wilson (9) 20
Reece Chatterfield (11) 21
Morgan Samuel Resnick (9) 21
Georgia Colgrave (11) 22
Callum Knight (10) 22
Isabella Cain (11) 23
Louis Rogers (11) 23
Joshua Green (10) 24
Adam Shotton (10) 24

Vincent Jordan (11)	25
Jessica Pedley (9)	25
Charis Bedford (11)	26
Rebecca Clark (10)	26
Saskia Lewis (8)	27
Maisie Taylor (8)	27
Lauren Hayes (10)	28
Katie-May Willdigg (10)	28
Isobelle Holmes (10)	29
Sophie Bird (8)	29
Kayleigh Barber (9)	30
Sophia Clark (10)	30
Adam Jones (10)	31
Conor Brown (10)	31
Daniel Arrowsmith (10)	32
Lucy Proverbs (8)	32
Ryan Lockett (11)	33
Ebony Broomfield (8)	33
Charlotte Williams (9)	34
Ellie Smith (10)	34
Owen Jake-Lloyd Bentley (10)	35
Grace Cain (10)	35
Adam Carless (9)	36
Ethan Lavender (9)	36
Jordan Tonks (9)	37
Jade-Olivia Smith (9)	37
Ben Morgan (10)	38
Grace Chaplain (10)	38
Abbie Rogers (10)	39
Stacey Bryan (10)	39
Bradley Matthews (11)	40
Kyan Hill (9)	40
Beatrice Rose Cain (10)	41
Lauryn May Sturgess (11)	41
James Sturgess (11)	42
Reid Glaze (11)	42
Paris Lauren Ramsay (7)	43
Zak Beebee (11)	43
Isabelle Ellis (9)	44
George Ellis (8)	44
Daniel Cooper (9)	45
Nathan Clarke (10)	45
Halle-Mae Johnson (7)	46
William Morris (10)	46
Lewis Bullock (9)	47
Ben Leighton (10)	47
Charlie Knobbs (10)	48
Jack Wood (9)	48
Kyrsten Faith Clarke (8)	49
Natasha Miller (10)	49
Georgia Green-Howe (11)	50
Carter Platt (9)	50
Katie West (10)	51
Rosy Jane Carr (9)	51
Alex Price (9)	52
Natasha Smith (11)	52
Georgia Sanford (10)	53
Jack Williams (11)	53
Eve Rollinson (8)	54
Sam Birch (9)	54
Adam Lewis (10)	55
Ella Rose Proverbs (9)	55
Kate Ordidge (10)	56
Ben Smith (9)	56
Harriet Slym (9)	57
Thomas Greensill (10)	57
Abbie Yates (10)	58
Abby Carr (10)	58
Chloe Hildreth (10)	59
Savannah Till (9)	59
George Bicknell (7)	59
Joseph Hughes (10)	60
Harriot Donnelly (8)	60
Sam Gadd (10)	60
Cameron Osborne (8)	61
Lily Jordan (8)	61
Thomas John Taylor (9)	61
Regan Smith (10)	62
Jack Hughes (8)	62
Max Wheeler (9)	62
Ben Colgrave (9)	63

Devonshire Junior School, Smethwick

Simran Kaur & Pavindeep Kaur (10)	63
Gursimran Kaur Sapra (8)	63
Arneet Uppal (8)	64
Gagandeep Singh Josan (7)	64
Davina Kaur Dhatt (8)	64
Simranjit Kaur (7)	65
Arundeep Kaur Dosanjh (7)	65

Elliemay Simcox (7) 65
Summer Strode (7) 66

Hall Green Primary School, West Bromwich
Thomas Belcher & Liam Felton 66
Iyesha Young (11) 66
Bethany Perry (10) 67
Shannon Rachel (10) 67

Harden Primary School, Walsall
Jack Hayward (9) 67
Charlotte Bellingham (8) 68
Holly Hall (7) 68
Kadie Johnson (7) 68
Charlie Fellows (8) 69
Tilly Mansell (8) 69
Hadia Rohail (7) 69
Sophie Middleton (8) 70
Hamza Rohail (9) 70
Matthew Foster (8) 70
Courtney Hall (9) 70
Natasha Westley (7) 71

King Henry VIII Preparatory School, Coventry
Nishant Rai (11) 71
Darshan Parekh (11) 72
Simran Banga (10) 73
Matthew Pandya (9) 74
Georgina Peake (10) 75
Nuwanji Amarasekera (11) 76
Elisabeth List (10) 77
James O'Leary (11) 78
Rebecca Aspinall (8) 78
Abbie Smith (10) 79
Harrison Waugh-Smith (8) 79
Anais Dosanj (10) 80
Sam Duckers (8) 80
Laura McTernan (11) 81
Aaron Hayre (10) 81
Jacob Knyspel (10) 82
Asmaa Ahmad (9) 82
Esha Joshi (9) 83
Sophie Oliver (10) 83
Jordan Parker (8) 84
Emriece Heer (11) 84

Oliver Kenyon (9) 85
Vedika Bedi (8) 85
Anastasia Jeffcoat (8) 86
Bethany Isard (10) 86
Deepinder Singh Dyal (9) 87
Caitlin Newport (9) 87
Alexandria Quinn (9) 88
William Astle (8) 88
Abigail Forsythe (8) 89
Toby Barham (8) 89
Emma McCabe (11) 90
Matthew Leatherdale (10) 90
George Wilkinson (11) 91
Dhruv Parekh (8) 91
Mary Gittens (10) 92
Karsha Dosanjh (9) 92
Anisha Gill-Saluja (10) 93
Havandeep Khatkar (9) 93
Sanjeet Chhokar (10) 94
Lauren Cox (9) 94
Jordan Gumbura (11) 95
Jacqueline Correa (8) 95
Visva Moorthy (11) 96
William Kelly (9) 96
Chelsey Johnson (10) 97
Lewis Mohindra (10) 97
Maariyah Sulaimaan (10) 98
Hannah Lucy Allen (11) 98
Josephine Kunc (9) 99
Amelia Moore (10) 99
Lyle Sargent (11) 100
Matthew Ratcliff (10) 100
Karam Singh Budwal (11) 101
Nayan Kyle Mistry (9) 101
Ria Sanghera (10) 102
Holly Slack (9) 102
Louisa Rowlands (10) 103
Kai Wayne-Wynne (9) 103
Ellena Marlow (9) 104
Imaan Turudi (9) 104
Ravi Parekh (10) 105
Ria Patel (9) 105
Simran Dhugga (10) 106
Daniel Mirfendereski (10) 106
Maadesh Raveendran (11) 107

Rachel Carron (9)	107
Kyra Jayde Jones (10)	108
Priya Bains (10)	108
Zahra Mushtaq (10)	109
Maisie Jane Taylor (11)	109
Esmé Dublin (10)	110
Ishita Jainer (9)	110
Caitlin Roper (11)	111
Harriet Morris (9)	111
Rahul Nayyar (10)	112
Harriet Rayner (9)	112
William Walker (9)	113
James Trigger (10)	113
Tom Lees (11)	114
Jay Jassi (9)	114
Ellinor Smith (8)	115
Samuel McLeod (9)	115
Keerat Dhadda (9)	116
Aum Sharda (9)	116
Alex McLean (10)	117
Matthew Small (11)	117
Michelle Panteli (10)	118
George Gawthorpe (9)	118
Amun Sangha (10)	119
Emma Lawrence (11)	119
Eve O'Sullivan (11)	120
Mayur Patel (9)	120
Muhammed Abid (11)	121
Shuva Ranjitkar (9)	121
Emily Moore (9)	122
Megan Bestard (10)	122
Layla Skinner (11)	123
Dani Haider (10)	123
Felix Marufu (11)	124
Davina Mistry (10)	124
Niamh Brennan (9)	125
Sahib Singh Takhar (10)	125
Joshua Aspinall (9)	126
Charlotte Cawley (10)	126
Ethan Latty (9)	127
Rachel Leigh (8)	127
Christie Neale (9)	128
Hannah Jane Kennedy (11)	128
Callum Durrant (11)	129
George Edwards (9)	129
Joshua Davenport (11)	130
Thomas Meynell (10)	130
William Collier (10)	131
Eleni Georgiades (10)	131
Cliona Anson-O'Connell (11)	132
James Maclean (10)	132
Kelechi Apakama (9)	133
Pavinder Suprai (11)	133
Jason Adams (8)	134
Sulayrnan Janjua (8)	134
Georgia Griffin (8)	135
Emily Nicholls (9)	135
Jasmine Close (9)	136
Karan Jutti (11)	136
Reanne Diane Smith (9)	137
Luke Manning (9)	137
Emily Smith (9)	138
Aasim Ahmed (8)	138
Gurjeevan Aujla (9)	138
Nikhil Trivedi (10)	139

Ravensmead Primary School, Bignall End

Oliver Walker (5)	139
Amelia Mayer (5)	140
Faith Bell (5)	140
Dominic Smith (5)	140
Rebecca Walley (7)	141
Thomas Mainwaring (6)	141
Jessica Mollart-Price (6)	141
Pippa Bradeley (4)	142

St Patrick's Catholic Primary School, Walsall

Awase Iyol (10)	142
Sebastian Kalicun (9)	142
Ayanna Kamose (10)	143
Evie Mansell (10)	143
Joao Cariata (10)	144
Libby Taylor (9)	144
Callum Marshall (9)	144
Sonia Chopra (9)	145
Levi Mason (10)	145
Nikisha Ward (10)	145
Courtney Ryan (10)	146
Todd Edmunds (9)	146

Becki Lang (10) 146
Springfield House Special School, Knowle
Sophie Fitzpatrick (11) 147
Thomas Harvey (10) 147
Peter Haden (10) 147
Ward End Primary School, Birmingham
Qasim Ali (10) 148
Tahir Mohammed (9) 148
Aisha Amjad (10) 149
Sara Said (10) 149
Tahreem Hussain (9) 150

The Poems

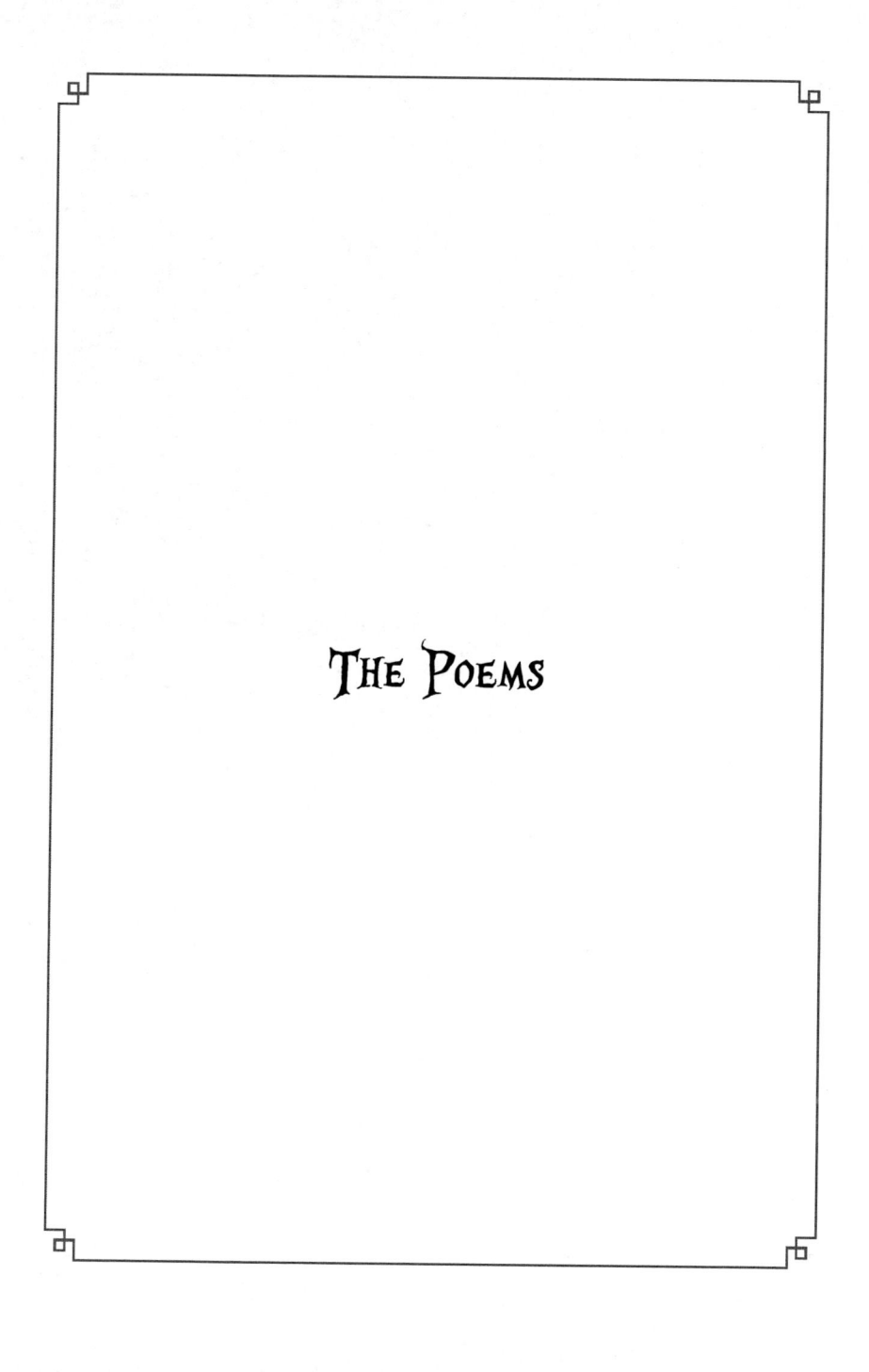

My Friends

My friend James
Likes to complain
He likes to play games
He runs down a lot of lanes.

My friend Ethan
Has been eaten
He is being defeated.

My friend Josh
Is very posh
He needs a really good wash
He'll probably have his in a load of dosh.

I have a friend called Shannon
She looks like a dragon
Lives in a wagon
Likes to look at cannons
She hates salmon.

My friend Bradley
Has a big sister called Amy
Lives in Cradley
He has a baby.

My friend Jack
Has a wonky back
Loves his cat
And is very fat.

Brad Willetts (11)
Blackheath Primary School, Rowley Regis

Friends!

Friends are upset
Friends are cheerful
Everyone rides
On top of my vehicle
We go around and around
On top of the world
And stars shine in the light
And stars shine on the sun.

Amy Longden (10)
Blackheath Primary School, Rowley Regis

My Family!

My family is extremely great
And one of my aunts is like Catherine Tate.
They have always been good enough for me
But only a couple are as good as can be.

Sweet is my wonderful, kind dad
But he can go raving mad!
My mum is as good as can be
And will love any cat she can see.
My brother annoyingly bugs me every single day
But really I don't care what he has to say.
My uncle is extremely nice
And loves any animals except for naughty little mice.
My aunt is very, very, very great
But she can be like Catherine Tate!

One of my aunts owns horses and a dog
But my other aunts can tear through a log.
I have two cats and so does my dad
And one of mine is extremely mad!
My aunt also owns another dog called Alfie
And he always loves to lick me.
She also owns two cats and two bunnies
Who cost her a lot of money.

Rachael Bradley (10)
Blackheath Primary School, Rowley Regis

My Friend Nat

I have a weird friend called Nat
Who is very, very fat.
She has a skinny pet cat
Who loves to lie on a mat.
Not forgetting her best friend Pat
Who always wears a silly hat.

Nat also loves to chase bats
And shows them how to eat rats.
She's still my weird friend
Who often drives me round the bend!

Chloe Millward (11)
Blackheath Primary School, Rowley Regis

My Friend Fiona Fry

My weird friend is called Fiona Fry,
And all she does is cry, cry, cry!
It is really boring but
If I was not her friend, she would cry about her foot.

Nobody knows why she cries,
She couldn't stop even if she really tries.
When the teacher asks why,
All she does is start to cry.

This is a mystery that needs to be solved,
If it doesn't she will probably go bald.
And if she does she will cry,
But I will just sit there and heave a huge, heavenly sigh.

Once before though, she was not at school,
And for once I could act really cool.
She came to the school gate,
She did not cry but said, 'I'm Fiona Fry!'

She ran off and started to giggle,
I was in such a muddle.
And that was the story of the girl who used to cry,
She is my weird friend and her name is Fiona Fry!

Shannon Kelly (10)
Blackheath Primary School, Rowley Regis

Friends Will Do Anything

Friends who are nice
Friends who are bad
Friends who would travel all around the world
Just to make you glad.
Friends who help you with your maths
Or help you revise for your SATs.
Friends are there for a reason
So don't go leaving them out.
They always have a smile on their face
So don't you wear them out.

Gemma Mittoo (10)
Blackheath Primary School, Rowley Regis

Our Pets

My friend's pig
It's called Snotters,
When he moves
You see his trotters.
My gran's cat
Moves around the room
And when she pounces
She goes zoom.
My brother's hamster,
He's called Twitch,
As he bites everyone,
We call him a witch.
My cousin's rabbit
Is called Bramble,
When he is scared
You see him scramble.
And my dog,
He's just a dog,
He likes his ball
And his best friend, a frog.

Kia Green (10)
Blackheath Primary School, Rowley Regis

My Pet

I have a pet
He's a bit of a dummy
That's because he's a mummy
All the friends he had
Are me, a bat and an old mat
His natural home is the shed
But when I'm at school
He goes to the pub and plays pool
Then when I come home
I go to the shed
Where he's lying there pretending to be dead
Then he has to be fed
Then it's time for bed!

Jack Bain (10)
Blackheath Primary School, Rowley Regis

My Dog Sharky

My dog Sharky, soft as a bottle of pop,
My dog Sharky, great at hip hop.

My dog Sharky, has shiny teeth and golden eyes,
My dog Sharky's favourite food is my mum's apple pies.

My dog Sharky's really fun,
Apart from when he just lays in the sun.

Clean up on aisle four,
My dog Sharky weed on the floor.

My dog Sharky's never late,
That's one of the things that makes him great.

My dog Sharky, takes the mick,
When he comes home and is sick.

My dog Sharky's really cool,
If you don't love him you're a fool.

My dog Sharky's really fat,
But that's because all day long he's sat.

Brandan Sabin (10)
Blackheath Primary School, Rowley Regis

The Sea

The sea clashes loudly with the warm sea air,
Showing its bare white teeth.
Coming closer, closer, closer, towards the barren shore,
Wiping away anything in its path,
Hacking away at the land.

Water rolls, giant waves head towards the sandy shore.
Thrusting to the rocky cliff face,
Cutting through the air,
Like a chainsaw through a tree.
Closer, closer. It's trying to claim me.

Now it's sunset upon the coast,
Calmer, calmer. The sea is becoming calmer.
Beautiful colours, ripples all around.
The sea's true nature, revealing itself to me.

Samuel Hingley (10)
Blackheath Primary School, Rowley Regis

My Pets!

Pets are the greatest thing ever,
Especially for my uncle Trevor.
If you are sad and lonely,
Go and get a pet, it will feel homely.

Smudge, who is my fluffy kitten,
She couldn't even fit into a mitten.
She is so cute and very crazy,
But when she's in bed, she'll be quite lazy.

The second one is called Midge,
He is always looking for food in the fridge.
He is quite old,
And he will always be big and bold.

I wish I had another cat,
One that isn't quite so fat.
I love cats very much,
That I will do as such,
Like I wrote this poem for you.

Jessica Whitehouse (11)
Blackheath Primary School, Rowley Regis

Barley

My mad dog Barley,
Should have named him Barmy,
He really likes to play,
But he has his days.
His name, Barley,
Coincidentally rhymes with Marley.
He goes for a walk
And acts like a dork!
His lukewarm fur
Could burn the sun!

Samuel Robson (10)
Blackheath Primary School, Rowley Regis

Different Friends

Friends that are happy.
Friends that are sad.
Friends that make you very glad.
Some that are ugly.
Some that are pretty.
Some that make you go round the city.
Friends that paint your faces.
Friends who go to different places.
Some go shopping with you.
Some that just care for you.
Friends that you see every day.
Friends that you see in May.
Some that like food.
Some that are just in the mood.
Friends that like the rain.
Friends that like to play games.
All my friends.
That all depends!

Charlotte Ockold (11)
Blackheath Primary School, Rowley Regis

The Monkey Who Said Hello

The monkey said hello,
Then he went yellow,
Multicoloured he went.

The monkey ran away,
Maybe he'll come back on Sunday.

We had a laugh
Although he smelt and needed a bath.
When he comes back he'll say hello
And then he will turn yellow.

Jesse Sherwood (10)
Blackheath Primary School, Rowley Regis

My Wonderful Friends

Fab friends, I've got two,
What about you?
Every day we play lots of games,
We find it fun, even when it rains!

My friends, my friends,
They are very special to me,
Even if one goes on . . . and on . . . and on
About Glee!

They aren't like sisters,
Click-clacking around in heels with blisters,
(Which causes a lot of pain).

My friends, my friends, with wonderful trends,
Some friends drive you around the bend,
Their fab clothes, they let you lend,
My friends, my friends,
My wonderful friends!

Alisha Subherwal (10)
Blackheath Primary School, Rowley Regis

Cow And Pig

I have a really fantastic but grubby-faced pet cow,
Who is literally here in the middle of nowhere right now.
She would really greedily eat you right up
In a nearly broken red, very large cup.
She would go off then whisper and natter to her friend the pig,
Not forgetting her name, Mig.
She is actually very kind,
Her lovely tasty food she loves to grind,
Now, let's rewind all her bad (very bad) memories.

Chloe Nock (10)
Blackheath Primary School, Rowley Regis

Cats!

Cats, cats
Anywhere
High or low
I don't know
Are they ugly
Or are they cute?
They might even
Give you a
Boot!

Jack James (10)
Blackheath Primary School, Rowley Regis

My Poor Dog

I had a dog who loved to bark,
I once took him to the park.
He loved it there but he fell in the pond,
In which he was rather fond.
My poor dog grew gills and fins,
Never again will he eat from the bins.

Jack William Powell (11)
Blackheath Primary School, Rowley Regis

Birds Of Prey

When you walk he's watching you.
When you sleep he's watching you.
When you play he's watching you.
He lives in treetops looking for food.
Be careful or he might eat you!

Drew Forrest (11)
Blackheath Primary School, Rowley Regis

Pets

P layful pets.
E at and eat.
T ime for tea.
S leep tight playful pets.

Hannah Jordan (10)
Blackheath Primary School, Rowley Regis

Global Warming

Earth's lungs are being made extinct
Losing lovely oxygen
Too much carbon dioxide
Beautiful animals being destroyed
Sea level rising
Causing floods
People dying
This is not good
Many homes gone forever
Help us or we'll be gone forever.

Callum Roadknight (8)
Brownhills West Primary School, Walsall

Changing Every Minute!

Changing every minute
Help!
Animals becoming extinct
Chopping down their homes
Forests losing their beauty
Planet getting hotter
Global warming
Dangerous floods
Help us now, you know you should!

Anais Morris (7)
Brownhills West Primary School, Walsall

Global Warming

Environment change
Burning, burning, planet burning
Foresters returning
Animals are rare
Their habitat will tear
Environment will change
Oxygen will no longer be made
Just yelp for some help!

Jack Cockayne (8)
Brownhills West Primary School, Walsall

Global Warming

The rainforest is being destroyed.
Animals are extinct,
People chopping down trees.
Animals losing their homes,
Too much global warming.
The planet is getting hotter,
We must act now!

Tanya Griffin (8)
Brownhills West Primary School, Walsall

Global Warming

Stop cutting trees.
We can't breathe.
Global warming.
Hotter and hotter.
Animals' homes destroyed.
Save the trees
Or you won't breathe.

Angel Steane (7)
Brownhills West Primary School, Walsall

Global Warming

Environment change
Planet getting hotter
Lungs of the Earth destroyed
Stop chopping trees
Oxygen to breathe
We need your help
So help us please!

Jessica Steane (8)
Brownhills West Primary School, Walsall

Global Warming

The Earth's lungs are being chopped down
So everyone will be low on the flow with oxygen.
If you raise the carbon dioxide higher
The world will be on fire.
The ice caps are melting
And there will be a belting with the floods.

Joe Hipwell (8)
Brownhills West Primary School, Walsall

The Awakening Of Spring

The awakening of spring,
Such a wonderful thing,
All the birds start to sing,
Waiting for what the new season will bring.

The birds fly high,
Swiftly up in the sky,
Knowing there spring will lie.

Winter's gone so do not fear,
Because you know spring is here.

Sunny Coco Marko Bennett (8)
Chad Vale Primary School, Edgbaston

Gondwanaland

O take me back to Gondwanaland,
before the terrible split.
When what was cloven,
was all interwoven,
and didn't differ a bit.

O dear cats of Gondwanaland,
now so vanished away.
I miss you so sorely,
I ache so rawly,
won't you come back one day?

Marsupials of Gondwanaland,
bigger than elephants too,
sloths and possums,
olontoglossums,
why do I dream of you?

Steamy heat of Gondwanaland,
when reptiles were the kings.
Life's so Malawian and neo-Australian,
and lots of nasty things.

O waft me away to Gondwanaland,
fly me away in the sky.
Forever I'm thrall to what's priminal,
until the day I die.

Amina Mekic (9)
Chad Vale Primary School, Edgbaston

Blue

Blue is the colour of waves in the sea,
Crashing against the giant rocks.

Blue is the colour of the beautiful sky,
With the lovely shining sun.

Blue is the colour of a beautiful bird,
Soaring through the sky.

Blue is the colour of a sapphire stone,
Shimmering in the deep, dark mine.

Leon Thomas (8)
Cheslyn Hay Primary School, Walsall

I Asked The Boy Who Cannot See . . .
(Based on 'I Asked The Little Boy Who Cannot See' by Anon)

I asked the boy who cannot see,
'What is colour like?'

'Why blue,' said he,
'Is like the relaxing, calm water
Swaying as the wind blows.'

'Red,' said he,
'Is like fireworks shooting up into the sky
And banging in the air.'

'Why white,' said he,
'Is like white tiger cubs
Playing in the icy cold snow.'

'And green,' said he,
'Is like the green grass swaying in the breeze
From side to side.'

'Why yellow,' said he,
'Is like the Easter chicks hatching on Easter Day
And chirping all day long.'

'Brown,' said he,
'Is like a chocolate Labrador barking at me
As he tries to chase me.'

'Why orange,' said he,
'Is the taste of a sour orange in my mouth.'

'Pink,' said he,
'Is like the smell of sweet roses in the field.'

'Purple,' said he,
'Is the smell of sweet lavender
Swaying in the field.'

'Why silver,' said he,
'Is like the diamond
Sparkling in the warm sunlight.'

Paige Stanyard (10)
Cheslyn Hay Primary School, Walsall

I Asked The Little Boy Who Cannot See . . .
(Based on 'I Asked The Little Boy Who Cannot See' by Anon)

I asked the little boy who cannot see,
'And what is colour like to you?'
'Why, red,' explained he,
'Red is a fiery angry colour,
Lava erupting as hot as the sun,
Ferocious and dangerous springs to mind.
Calmness and coldness, that is blue,
Water trickling down a stream,
Clear blue skies on a dry, hot morning.
And yellow is like the sand on holiday,
Stars as bright as a light in the darkest of nights.
And pink is a flamingo,
Elegant and proud, foxgloves growing out of the ground,
A newborn piglet,
Cute and cuddly.
That purple must be plums and grapes,
Fresh and sweet, mountains at dawn
And orange is a sunset,
Street lamps glowing like the boiling hot sun
And a juicy orange.
White is snow, winter fluffy clouds
Like candyfloss, when you sleep at night a pleasant dream.
Silver is ice and frost,
Diamonds that glimmer in the glistening light,
A feather falling down from the sky,
Last but not least,
Brown is a tree trunk,
A puppy as sweet as chocolate
And mud that lies on the ground.'

Georgia Barber (11)
Cheslyn Hay Primary School, Walsall

Red

Red is the colour of a bright red rose
Red is the colour of a devil
Red is a beautiful colour
Red is a colour on the England flag.

Olivia Woolley (8)
Cheslyn Hay Primary School, Walsall

Space Football

There was a sight,
When the Space Marines
Came out

Then there was a fright,
When the Dark Lords
Arrived

Unfortunately,
The Space Marines
Were driven off the ball
Because they were a shambles!

Peep! the whistle goes,
The Dark Lords had
Taken a few blows
But they were better all along

Back in the changing rooms
The Dark Lords had a fight.
But all you could hear
Was a loud boom!

In the second half,
It was very peculiar
Because a calf
Walked onto the pitch!

It took a long time
For the stewards
To move the calf because
One of them was a titch!

Tomas Ethan Mayo (8)
Cheslyn Hay Primary School, Walsall

All The Colours Of The Rainbow

Red is for a hot, fiery balloon escaping into the sky
Blue is for the deep blue sea
Green is the thick grass of Heaven
Yellow is for the brightness of the sun
Violet is for the violet flowers that shine at me when I run.

Ellison Yates (8)
Cheslyn Hay Primary School, Walsall

Ten Spotty Dogs

(Inspired by 'Ten Little Schoolboys' by A A Milne)

Ten spotty dogs sitting in a line,
One went for a nap and then there were nine.

Nine spotty dogs heading for the gate,
One went through and then there were eight.

Eight spotty dogs wondering what it would be like in Heaven,
One went up and then there were seven.

Seven spotty dogs doing loads of kicks,
One went to do licks and then there were six.

Six spotty dogs doing loads of dives,
One went for a swim and then there were five.

Five spotty dogs tearing letters,
One went to see some more and then there were four.

Four spotty dogs looking at a bee,
One went to eat a pea and then there were three.

Three spotty dogs jumping in a shoe,
One went to say boo and then there were two.

Two spotty dogs saying the word none,
One went to be gone and then there was one.

One spotty dog looking in the pond,
Then he ran away to his owner and then there were none!

So there were no spotty dogs,
Tomorrow they will play again!

Elle Mae Phillips (7)
Cheslyn Hay Primary School, Walsall

The Rainbow Flowers

Roses are red
Violets are blue
You can see it in a view
While you eat an ice cream too.
In the burning sunlight
Come and have some glorious fun.

James Hickson-Akehurst (8)
Cheslyn Hay Primary School, Walsall

My Journey Through The Seasons

Spring
In the spring the flowers grow,
But in winter they're covered in snow.
I saw the monkeys swinging from tree to tree
And the colourful birds flying above me,
'What beautiful birds!' I cried,
And carried along on my journey.

Summer
In summer the sun shines
And the furry animals swing from the vines.
Then I saw some birds
Swoop down from the sky,
'Are you sure they're not dive-bombers?' I asked
And I carried on my way.

Autumn
In autumn the leaves fall off the trees
And I start to get frightened . . .
Oh please, oh please,
Find me somewhere to stay.
'I'll perish,' I cried
And carried along on my way.

Winter
Now I have to battle,
Through the tough winter snow
And I haven't got a clue,
Where I have to go.

Morgan Owen (9)
Cheslyn Hay Primary School, Walsall

Hamster

H e is a little biting hamster.
A t midnight he runs on his wheel.
M y hamster is soft and cuddly.
S o I don't know what to call him.
T hrows his food pot everywhere.
E vil little hamster who will you bite next?
R uns everywhere in his wheel, oh where is he?

Jamie Haldron (9)
Cheslyn Hay Primary School, Walsall

What Shall I Do?

This poem's really bugging me
I don't know what to do
You may not believe it but it's not for me
It's for my brilliant primary school.

What shall I do on this next line?
Hmm, perhaps something about me
I want it to be really divine
But actually it's not (that's between you and me).

What shall I put down, what shall I put down?
I don't have a clue
And on my face lies a frown
Oh what shall I do?

Let me see, what shall I do next
To gain something for school?
I'll really try to do my best
Oh I am no fool.

I really want to get
This poem in a book
But maybe they won't let me
But I still want a look at that book.

Perhaps I should close this poem to an end
And wait for next week (when I'm at school)
I'm going to play outside, yahoo
But my simple question is . . . oh,
What shall I do?

Sinali Gunarathne (9)
Cheslyn Hay Primary School, Walsall

Weather

W ash out
E ye of the storm
A rctic winds
T hunder and lightning
H ail storms
E ast winds may blow, we shall have snow
R ainbow high up in the sky.

Amy-Jo Bickley (10)
Cheslyn Hay Primary School, Walsall

I Asked The Boy Who Cannot See . . .

(Based on 'I Asked The Little Boy Who Cannot See' by Anon)

'What is colour like?'

'Green is a leaf, simple yet graceful,
Soaring through the air like a plane,
Twirling, dancing, amazing!

Red is a ruby dragon, gliding through the damp air,
Its heart filled with the deepest rage,
Its fire incinerating forests, turning them to dust.

Pink is the softest wool, pressing against my rosy cheek,
Soothing all pain as well as hurt.

Purple is a horrible wound, burning, burning with pain,
Not only hurting my body but hurting my mind,
Forcing me to lose confidence as if it is being sucked out of me.

Yellow is a lightning bolt racing across the sky,
Like children racing on a playground,
Striking all in its path, nothing can stop this mighty wonder.

White is an enormous polar bear
Galloping across the sheet white ice, ready to hunt.

Black is a pitch-black night as cold as ice
Lasting forever while all nature softly sleeps.

Blue is the enormous sky with fluffy white clouds
Like sheep drifting around, looking up at the sky is amazing, says I.'

Joshua Harrison (10)
Cheslyn Hay Primary School, Walsall

People

Some people talk and talk.
Some people never say a thing.
Some people stare at you
And we can also sing.

Some people giggle and giggle
And some just want to cry.
Some people hold your hand
And love fills the sky.

Matthew Wilson (9)
Cheslyn Hay Primary School, Walsall

The Boy Who Cannot See . . .
(Based on 'I Asked The Little Boy Who Cannot See' by Anon)

I asked the boy who cannot see,
'Describe the colours on a bee.'

'Yellow tastes of sour spray and stings your eyes until it dies.
Scolding heat that always burns everything to cinders,' said he.

'Black is the colour of evil creatures that are hooded like ghosts.
Soul-sucking monsters that penetrate dreams
Transforming them into nightmares.

So they are the colours of a bee described with my opinion.'

'What are the colours of the sea?' I said to he.

'Why the sea is blue like the sky that forces coldness through you.'
He came, 'Waves of white bring delight to children on the beach.
Sandy brown, can bring a frown to the faces of some people.

That's the sea, described like the bee, all from my point of view.'

'Just one more thing, I would like to add my friend,
Tell me what colour is the night?'

'The night is purple like UV light that replaces the sky.
Silver lights all around the stars that watch over us.
Fiery streaks of meteors that burn up gradually,' he replied to me.

'And that is the night full of delight described to you from me.'

That's the story of what I asked the boy who cannot see.

Reece Chatterfield (11)
Cheslyn Hay Primary School, Walsall

The Fat Rat

There once was a rat,
Who was very fat,
When he jumped in the sewer pipes,
He got washed away in the sewer.

Soon he was in the tub,
Then he went to the pub,
He ordered a cake,
That was easy to bake.

Morgan Samuel Resnick (9)
Cheslyn Hay Primary School, Walsall

I Asked The Little Boy Who Cannot See . . .

(Based on 'I Asked The Little Boy Who Cannot See' by Anon)

I asked the boy who cannot see,
'And what is colour like?'
'Why green,' said he,
'Is the damp, soft grass,
Tickling my toes as I pass,
With a fresh smell,
Of newly mown grass by the well,
Trees blowing in the silent breeze,
And the pollen makes me sneeze!

Yellow is warm,
Lying on your lawn,
The sun in your eyes,
The tulips I despise,
Soft, velvet petals - silky,
Aahh, a banana milkshake - milky,
Cold and fresh, the best!

Pink is flamingos,
By the water that flows,
Soft, pink, light,
Elegant but no flight,
Candyfloss melts in your mouth,
No good for your health!

Colours are my favourite things!'

Georgia Colgrave (11)
Cheslyn Hay Primary School, Walsall

I Asked The Boy Who Cannot See . . .

(Based on 'I Asked The Little Boy Who Cannot See' by Anon)

I asked the boy who cannot see,
'What is colour like?'

'Pink is like candyfloss that goes around in a machine.
Red is like fire that warms your face.
White is like an ice cream but freezes your tongue.
Blue is like the sea that is wet and cold and tickles my feet.
Brown is like a chocolate Labrador that is smooth and silky.'

Callum Knight (10)
Cheslyn Hay Primary School, Walsall

I Asked The Boy Who Cannot See . . .

(Based on 'I Asked The Little Boy Who Cannot See' by Anon)

I asked the little boy who cannot see,
'And what is colour like?'
'Why, pink,' said he,
'Is like the sweet, dissolving feel of candyfloss on your tongue,
The rubbery feel of a fat pig's blubbery belly like a huge pillow.'

'O right, so what is purple?' I asked.
'Well purple is the relaxing scent of lavender swaying you to sleep,
Purple is the beautiful blanket of heather crawling up the rockside.'

'So tell me more, what is blue?' questioned I.
'Well, I think of blue as the cool, calm sea
Trickling through your toes,
Blue is the smoothness of bluebells, as beautiful as a diamond.'

'So what is red?' I said.
'Why, red is the sweet scent of love-filled roses
Posted to your heart from your lover, just as special as a kiss,
Red is the poppy, giving you a minute's silence for Remembrance.'

'So what is yellow to you?' I wondered.
'In my mind yellow is the scorching sun
Giving you a golden tone to your skin,
On the warmest day of summer,
Yellow is the beautiful butterfly flapping on your cheeks,
Like a bird's feather tickling your cheek.'

Isabella Cain (11)
Cheslyn Hay Primary School, Walsall

I Asked The Boy Who Cannot See . . .

(Based on 'I Asked The Little Boy Who Cannot See' by Anon)

'What is colour like?'
'Green, green is a juicy apple lying on the grass.
Blue, blue is the sky shining through clouds.
Red, red is flames burning high in the sky.
Pink, pink are the roses, soft and silky.
Purple, thunderstorms like a gun in action.
Yellow, yellow are the bees buzzing with madness.
White, white are the fluffy sheep getting shaved.'

Louis Rogers (11)
Cheslyn Hay Primary School, Walsall

Double The Trouble

My little puppy is quite bold,
She doesn't always do as she is told.

My little sister is much the same,
She often ruins my favourite game.

They make a lot of noise,
And they've both chewed my toys.

The cables are in muddles,
And they both jump in muddy puddles.

Running here, chasing there,
Barking and shouting everywhere.

Keeping the house nice and neat,
Is not an easy feat.

'Settle down,' Mum will shout,
As they race and chase about.

My puppy chews my socks,
And the cupboards need locks.

I never get to watch the telly,
And they both can be smelly.

But I suppose they are both sweet,
Especially when they're both asleep.

Joshua Green (10)
Cheslyn Hay Primary School, Walsall

I Asked The Little Boy Who Cannot See . . .

(Based on 'I Asked The Little Boy Who Cannot See' by Anon)

I asked the little boy who cannot see,
'And what is colour like?'
'What, red?' asked he,
'Red is danger, like the sound of screaming echoing round the cliff.
Coldness is blue, the bitter cold and snow hammering down like tiny demons.
Then yellow is a butterfly dancing in the wind like a ballerina.
Pink is love, care and softer bits like all around
And last of all a white leopard is silver venturing in a snow storm.'

Adam Shotton (10)
Cheslyn Hay Primary School, Walsall

I Asked The Boy Who Cannot See . . .

(Based on 'I Asked The Little Boy Who Cannot See' by Anon)

I asked the boy who cannot see
What colours he could sense like me
Quietly he replied,
'I sense the colours passing by.'

'What is red?' I asked softly.
'Why red is an evil dragon swooping in the sky
Attacking villages and devastating crop lands.

And blue is calm.
It is a rippling ocean quietly in the light of the moon,
And gracefully travelling on and on.

Yellow is a butterfly ever venturing through a dreamland
Fluttering over a peaceful brook.

And green is a bed of grass covered in a duvet of dew
Glimmering in the moonlight.

Silver is a sugar-frosted garden encrusted with shattered glass
And diamonds growing from trees.

And brown is the creamy texture of freshly made smooth chocolate
Melting in my mouth.
That is what colour is like,' he replied.

Vincent Jordan (11)
Cheslyn Hay Primary School, Walsall

Best Friends

B eautiful smile my friends have
E very time you're down they're always there for you
S ometimes very mad but whatever happens I'm not sad
T imes they're crazy, times they're lazy

F riends are thoughtful for you and others
R ound the corner or far away
I ncredible heroes they are today
E xciting adventures waiting to begin
N ever let me down
D efinitely my friends
S o never forget.

Jessica Pedley (9)
Cheslyn Hay Primary School, Walsall

I Asked The Boy Who Could Not See . . .
(Based on 'I Asked The Little Boy Who Cannot See' by Anon)

I asked the boy who could not see,
'What is red?'
'Why red is a sweet glossy apple,
Growing on an old tree,
In the cold autumn wind.'

I asked the boy who could not see,
'What is blue?'
'Why blue is the calm ocean,
Making chilly diminutive waves,
While young children play.'

I asked the boy who could not see,
'What is yellow?'
'Why yellow is the golden sand,
Crumbling into tiny pieces,
Tickling my warm toes.'

I asked the boy who could not see,
'What is green?'
'Why green is veiny leaves, hanging from newborn trees
Rustling loudly like an old lion roaring,
Falling and falling to the hard ground.'

Charis Bedford (11)
Cheslyn Hay Primary School, Walsall

I Asked The Boy Who Cannot See . . .
(Based on 'I Asked The Little Boy Who Cannot See' by Anon)

I asked a boy who cannot see,
'What is a colour like?'

'Pink,' he said,
'Pink is the sweetness of candyfloss that melts in your mouth
And red is the beautiful smell of roses lingering up my nose,
Yellow is the bright sun shining down,
Blue is the sky on sunny days,
White is the coldness of the glittering snow, as cold as ice,
Green is the fresh smell of lawn mowed grass in the morning,
Orange is the sweet taste of oranges, as juicy as grapefruit.'

Rebecca Clark (10)
Cheslyn Hay Primary School, Walsall

A Dragon's Life

I am a sleek black dragon with eyes of forest-green,
My wings are strong and bat-like,
They carry me on the wind,
I slice through the air like a blade,
I swoop, I race, I dive,
I can breathe fire, as hot as a volcano,
I can shoot electricity from my horns.

I race with my friends around the cliff face,
We love every turn,
I am so quick I beat them every time,
I gambol down the hills with them,
It's fun being a dragon, to fly using all my powers.

We only come out at night, when it's darkest,
The darkness is our cloak, protecting us from harm,
The word 'dragon' has been feared for many years,
We live in fear of being discovered,
By humans, who will wipe us out.

So now you've read my poem,
It's all about dragons, and how we live and survive,
But you don't have to be frightened of us,
Because we're also afraid of you.

Saskia Lewis (8)
Cheslyn Hay Primary School, Walsall

Blue

Blue is the colour of the crystal-blue
And clear deep blue sea
Blue is the colour of the sparkling deep blue sky
That twinkles in the moonlight
Blue is the colour of a shiny balloon
That's floated away in the moonlight
Blue is the colour of a beautiful raindrop
Drifting down from the sky
Blue is the colour of a new and shiny coat
Perfect for splashing in the rain
Blue is the colour of the icing on a birthday cake
For someone very special.

Maisie Taylor (8)
Cheslyn Hay Primary School, Walsall

I Asked The Little Boy Who Cannot See . . .
(Based on 'I Asked The Little Boy Who Cannot See' by Anon)

I asked the little boy who cannot see,
'And what are colours like?'
He looked at me with his empty eyes then answered,
'Why orange, orange is the colour of warmth,
When you feel like your skin is an open flame,
And about to burst into a million pieces.
Red is the colour of panic,
When you feel like your heart is going to break through your chest,
Then escape with every single secret.
White is the colour of peace,
It makes you feel warm, fuzzy
And all of your emotions pour into your mouth
Then make you feel relaxed.
Blue is the colour of the wind,
When you can feel the wind rushing in-between your hair,
And clinging to your arms and legs
Trying to bring you upwards.
Lastly,' whispered the little boy,
'Yellow is the colour of happiness,
It makes you feel like jumping up and laughing all day long,
Then going into restful sleep.'

Lauren Hayes (10)
Cheslyn Hay Primary School, Walsall

The Little Boy Who Can't See
(Based on 'I Asked The Little Boy Who Cannot See' by Anon)

I asked the boy who cannot see,
'And what is colour like?'
'Why, grey,' said he,
'Is like the sound of thundering grey cloud
Crashing against the white,
And an elephant trumpeting from his trunk.
Orange is like the tiger with a roar
That booms out of his bloodthirsty mouth
And the sun warming us like an oven.
Black is like the night sky with booming lights from the stars
And a silky panther crawling slyly through the bushes.'

Katie-May Willdigg (10)
Cheslyn Hay Primary School, Walsall

I Asked The Little Boy Who Cannot See . . .
(Based on 'I Asked The Little Boy Who Cannot See' by Anon)

I asked the little boy who cannot see,
'And what is colour like?'
'Why, white,' said he,
'It's like the snow as it feathers your face.

But red too,' said he, 'also,
It's like the red sky at night,
Is always shepherd's delight,
Red is also the colour of blood
That floods out from your knee when you've grazed it.'

'What about green?'
'Green is like the swishing trees
Making me go all dizzy
And the soft and smooth banana leaves
And the rough veins on them.'

'Don't forget gold and silver.'
'Well, gold, gold is the sun that keeps us boiling hot on a sunny day
And keeps the sky nice and bright.

Silver, silver is the moonlight that shines on the mountains
At night and the ice cobwebs and the glimmering dresses in the spotlight.'

Isobelle Holmes (10)
Cheslyn Hay Primary School, Walsall

My Dog

My dog is crazy,
My dog is lazy,
My dog bites old ladies.

My dog wakes up at ten o'clock
When I'm sleeping,
My dog bites in the noon
Until I pop.

My dog can shiver and fight
But he's out of my sight.

My dog is mad
But I'm glad I'm alright.

Sophie Bird (8)
Cheslyn Hay Primary School, Walsall

Animals

Cats, cats
Furry little fuzzball
Cats, cats
Curl up by the fire

Dogs, dogs
Jumping up the cupboard doors
Dogs, dogs
Cuddle up with you

Hamsters, hamsters
In your little plastic cages
Hamsters, hamsters
You're little balls of fluff

Pigs, pigs
Jump in muddy puddles
Pigs, pigs
Rough, pink, muddy animals

Animals, animals
Love them all
Animals, animals
Are all outside your door.

Kayleigh Barber (9)
Cheslyn Hay Primary School, Walsall

I Asked The Boy Who Cannot See . . .

(Based on 'I Asked The Little Boy Who Cannot See' by Anon)

I asked the boy who cannot see,
'What is a colour like?'
'Why, red,' said he,
'Is like a little ladybird, as small as a pebble and smooth,
Blue, is a blueberry, small and sour like a lemon.
Pink, nail polish, runny like water but smells like paint,
Also watermelon, inside squashy like a sponge.
Yellow, stars, glittering in the moonlight.
White, swans, vicious but elegant,
Some snow, soft and cold like ice.
Green, frogs, wet and slimy like whipped egg.'

Sophia Clark (10)
Cheslyn Hay Primary School, Walsall

The Adventure Of The Aeroplane

Today's the day the aeroplane,
The aeroplane went and flew,
But as he climbed altitude,
His engine went and blew.

He came down like a rocket,
A rocket he was then,
But as he nearly smashed to pieces,
He pulled up and started again.

When he reached the clouds,
The clouds so high in the air,
Some Germans swooped down,
But luckily it was only a pair.

He dodged them like a football player,
He dodged them as fast as a bee,
He got away just in time,
And got home just for tea.

I parked up in my hangar,
And got ready for tea,
Mmmm, my favourite,
Petrol just for me!

Adam Jones (10)
Cheslyn Hay Primary School, Walsall

I Asked The Little Boy Who Could Not See . . .

(Based on 'I Asked The Little Boy Who Cannot See' by Anon)

I asked the little boy who could not see,
'And what is colour like?'

'Why, red,' said he,
'The meaning of danger with a flare bursting in the sky.
The colour of love in the air.
Purple is the colour of the peaceful lavender flower
With a sweet scent filling the land
And the rough carpet of heather scratching my feet.

Blue is the colour of a racing waterfall
Rushing over the rocks or the calm lakes, still as a mirror.'

Conor Brown (10)
Cheslyn Hay Primary School, Walsall

My Magic Carpet

I found a magic carpet,
It was hidden in my room,
Amongst all the clutter,
It was next to a broom.

I sat on the carpet,
It slowly began to rise.
It started moving quickly,
It came as a big surprise.

My carpet flew out of my window
And headed for the park.
The wind was going through my hair,
I could hear the dogs bark.

My carpet turned around
And headed for my house.
It shot through the window,
As quiet as a mouse.

I jumped off the carpet
And landed in my bed,
With lots of excitement
Going through my head.

Daniel Arrowsmith (10)
Cheslyn Hay Primary School, Walsall

One Day

One summer day,
I went outside to play.
One winter's night,
My sister gave me a fright.
I was twirling round and round,
Then *bang!* I hit the ground.
I hurt my head,
Then I was sent to bed.
One day I lost my dog,
The next day I found him in a fog.
One freezing day,
I had to go away.

Lucy Proverbs (8)
Cheslyn Hay Primary School, Walsall

I Asked The Boy Who Cannot See . . .
(Based on 'I Asked The Little Boy Who Cannot See' by Anon)

I asked the boy who couldn't see,
'What is colour like?'
He told me that red was blood spilling out of a dragon's heart
While flames came burning out, taking everything in its path,
Like a black hole.
Green is a leaf that gets blown off the tree,
Green is the newly cut grass.
Pink is romantic love,
A soft fluffy colour like candyfloss,
Pink also is bright tops as people walk down the road,
As pink cars pass them.
Blue is crystal lakes,
They gently stroll into the rivers on the way home to the sea.
Purple is evil like a storm that rips and tears people's houses apart.
The same as yellow, a really warm colour,
Roasting by the fire on a freezing cold day.
Brown is chocolate like a Labrador
And Cadbury's chocolate that we eat.
White and black, the opposite,
Icy paths and a pitch-black night.

Ryan Lockett (11)
Cheslyn Hay Primary School, Walsall

Dark Blue

Dark blue is the colour of the thunder in the sky,
As it strikes down onto the trees,
Only the ones that are high,
The birds in the treetop in their stick built nest,
With all the birds round there just for a feast,
Dark blue is the colour of the stars shining bright,
Only in the really dark night,
Dark blue is the colour of when you are sad,
When tears drip down your face it feels so sad,
Dark blue is the colour of the deep blue sea,
That fish swim in when they are not looking at me,
Dark blue is the colour of the first page of a book,
That looks really good, so take a look.

Ebony Broomfield (8)
Cheslyn Hay Primary School, Walsall

The Old Abandoned Castle

A long time ago,
There was a large jagged hill,
On that large jagged hill
There is an old abandoned castle.

In that old abandoned castle,
There is a weird cellar,
In that there is
A dead skeleton.

It shook and it rattled,
Through the heavy wind,
If you ever saw it,
The jaws would drop and scare you away.

Also in the castle there is
A bedroom that nobody is fond of,
The curtains clack,
The bedclothes make such a racket.

What am I going to do?
What's coming at me?
Argh!

Charlotte Williams (9)
Cheslyn Hay Primary School, Walsall

I Asked The Little Boy Who Cannot See . . .

(Based on 'I Asked The Little Boy Who Cannot See' by Anon)

I asked the boy who cannot see,
'And what is colour like?'

'Why red,' he said,
'Is like fireworks shooting up into the night sky
And bursting with spectacular colours
And the smell of the match being blown out after.

Yellow is like a butterfly's wings
When it gently sways through the wind
When the delicate wings flap it's like someone's heartbeat.

Green is a freshly mowed field full of pretty birds
Tweeting as the grass sways left and right.'

Ellie Smith (10)
Cheslyn Hay Primary School, Walsall

I Asked The Little Boy Who Couldn't See . . .

(Based on 'I Asked The Little Boy Who Cannot See' by Anon)

I asked the little boy who cannot see,
'And what are the colours you'd like to be?'

'Oh, what I'd like to be,
Why red,' said he,
'The flaming firework higher than me,
A vicious dragon roaring out its fire
As its wings flap it gets higher and higher,
A beautiful poppy to remember our soldiers
And their trenches are bigger than boulders.

Orange is the sun with its warmth and its glow
With the wind it's strong and it gives us a blow,
Orange is the colour of an angry tiger, as it hunts its prey
But they might be extinct tomorrow or today.

Blue is the colour of the calm sea,
As beautiful as can be
But sometimes it rushes with a big push
Like an adrenaline rush,
It makes a massive noise as it goes whoosh.'

Owen Jake-Lloyd Bentley (10)
Cheslyn Hay Primary School, Walsall

My Scrummy Yummy Cupcake

My scrummy yummy cupcake,
Bake it in your break.

A scrummy yummy cupcake,
Not long to make.

A scrummy yummy cupcake,
Sprinkle it with Flake.

Take it to your mom,
Your scrummy yummy cupcake.

Now it's the end of break,
Where is my cupcake?
My mom has eaten
My scrummy yummy cupcake!

Grace Cain (10)
Cheslyn Hay Primary School, Walsall

I Am A Shark

I'm in the sea,
I live in the dark,
I eat fish for my breakfast, lunch and dinner,
I am a shark.

There are hammerheads, black tips, tiger sharks and more,
But the best of the lot is the great white of course.

I glide through the water with the greatest of ease,
Dipping and diving and doing as I please,
I'm always on the lookout for something to eat,
Fish are great but humans are always a treat.

I have great big jaws and razor-sharp teeth,
I am pleased to meet you, my name is Keith,
I detect blood in the water and have a sensitive nose,
I am quite big and scary I suppose.

You know all about me now, so what do you think?
Could you be my friend, just give me a wink,
Do you fancy a swim in the deep blue sea?
If so, turn into a shark and come and join me.

Adam Carless (9)
Cheslyn Hay Primary School, Walsall

Football

F ouls
O pportunity from a penalty
O ffside in the box
T hrow in
B ad challenge
A ttacking
L acking of speed
L osing

P layers
L ast in the league
A big football legend
Y oung talented 16-year-old player
E nd of the match
R eferee I've broken my leg.

Ethan Lavender (9)
Cheslyn Hay Primary School, Walsall

No School Today

Hip hip hooray
No school today
The weatherman said there's snow on the way

So put on your hats, coats and gloves
Let's get in the garden
And have some fun

Build a snowman big and tall
Or build a snowman fat and small
Make snowballs one by one
Then throw them until they've gone.

Fingers and toes are tingling
Nose is frozen too
Nearly time to go inside
Because we're turning blue

Water bottles waiting
Warm towels wrapped around my feet
Thinking about my snowman
The day has been a treat.

Jordan Tonks (9)
Cheslyn Hay Primary School, Walsall

Beautiful Huskies

B eautiful baby huskies are so adorable
E ek, I'm scared of huskies . . . no need to be
A m I scared of huskies? No!
U mbrellas keep them dry
T he UK sells huskies, buy one or ten
I 've got an amazing cuddly toy dog called Wuskey!
F luffy huskies never break my heart
U nforgettable dogs they are
L ovely huskies have to live

H usky, husky, you're the best
U nited Kingdom sells the best huskies
S o super, so cool, huskies rule
K iller dogs, killer dogs, go away and leave my husky alone today
Y ou can get amazing, beautiful, gorgeous dogs . . . *huskies!*

Jade-Olivia Smith (9)
Cheslyn Hay Primary School, Walsall

I Asked The Little Boy Who Cannot See . . .
(Based on 'I Asked The Little Boy Who Cannot See' by Anon)

'What is colour like?'

'Red is volcanoes bursting with rage, emitting blazing infernos,
Powerfully incinerating all in its path.

Blue is a serene river refreshing vegetation,
Calmly gushing down an infinitely tall valley.

Green is a lonely leaf withered with old age,
Sadly dancing in the wind like a majestic bird soaring in the sky.

Yellow is lightning, almost invisible as it travels at the speed of sound,
Electrifying any object with a single touch.

Pink is love, spreading cheer all around like a celebration,
Giving everyone a safe, happy feeling.

White is snow, as soft as wool gently descending from the sky,
Covering a pond with an icy sheet.

Black is a panther, as hidden as its own shadow,
Mysteriously travelling through the night in search of unsuspecting prey.'

Ben Morgan (10)
Cheslyn Hay Primary School, Walsall

My Dog Flo

I have a dog called Flo
She loves to play in the snow
She follows me here
She follows me there.
Wherever I go
She jumps up and down
Round in the town
Without a frown.
She hates getting washed, rub, rub, rub
Without a doubt.
Flo licks your face up and down, yuck!
She has lots of hair falling out the sky
Round and round like a fly.
Flo is a beagle, a lovely breed
She has lots of colours, really indeed.

Grace Chaplain (10)
Cheslyn Hay Primary School, Walsall

I Asked The Boy Who Can't See . . .

(Based on 'I Asked The Little Boy Who Cannot See' by Anon)

I asked the boy who can't see,
'And what is colour like?'
'Why, white,' said he,
'Is the crunching sound of my tiny feet
Sinking into the freezing snow,
It's also a snow leopard's fur,
As comforting as my first teddy bear.
The sea is blue with the waves dangerously crashing,
Against the soft sand,
Like a tiger's teeth eating up its prey.
Red is a fire-breathing dragon
Roaring at me with its breath as hot as a fire,
Burning up gnarled wood
And the feeling of the poppies in my heart
From when the brave soldiers fought in the war.
Green is the smell that lingers in my nose
From the freshly mowed grass,
Swaying in the summer breeze.'

Abbie Rogers (10)
Cheslyn Hay Primary School, Walsall

I Asked A Boy Who Cannot See . . .

(Based on 'I Asked The Little Boy Who Cannot See' by Anon)

I asked the boy who cannot see,
'What is colour like?'
'Why, orange,' spoke he,
'It's the beautiful orange sunset,
And also brown is a puppy, well a pet.
Black is the colour of the night sky
And yellow is the beach where people pass by.
Blue is the colour of the wet sea
And, why, green is a little pea.
Pink is a watery, juicy melon
But also red is the ferocious fireworks
That are red and bright.
White is a soft fluffy cloud
That you lie on every night.'

Stacey Bryan (10)
Cheslyn Hay Primary School, Walsall

I Asked The Little Boy Who Cannot See . . .
(Based on 'I Asked The Little Boy Who Cannot See' by Anon)

I asked the little boy who cannot see,
'And what is colour?'

'Well green is like a freshly mowed garden,
It is like a slimy frog.

Red is a little rose in a gigantic open place,
It is a flare bright and loud,
It is the colour of a dragon's flame, the colour of it.

White is like a snow leopard or a snow tiger,
It is ice, you go to an ice skating rink on the cold ice
And white chocolate,
The frost on a spider's web, the cold breeze in the air.

And pink, a small rose but very lively,
A sweet fragrance in the air,
A pig in a hut and a unicorn,
A magical creature with a horn on its head
And not to forget sweet candyfloss, lots of sugar on it.'

Bradley Matthews (11)
Cheslyn Hay Primary School, Walsall

Football

I'm the striker of my team
And playing professional football is my dream.
We play a game of 7 a-side,
The offside we need not abide.

When I kick the ball
I'm bound to score,
Na, na, na, na, na, na, na!

I'm not fussed about the riches and fame,
I just want to win all of my games.
When I want to play well and I'm eager to win,
I make sure I score and wear a big grin.

When I kick a ball
I'm bound to score,
Na, na, na, na, na, na, na!

Kyan Hill (9)
Cheslyn Hay Primary School, Walsall

Go Down To The Jungle

Go down to the jungle . . .

Mike the monkey
Is known for eating grapes.
With his cheeky little smile
He loves chasing apes.

Hilary the hippo
Is known for playing football.
The only problem is
He is extremely small.

Gill the giraffe
Is known for his extremely long tail.
His favourite hobby is
Delivering the mail.

Leo the lion
Is known for playing cricket.
His only problem is
He is rubbish at hitting the wicket.

Beatrice Rose Cain (10)
Cheslyn Hay Primary School, Walsall

I Asked The Little Boy Who Cannot See . . .

(Based on 'I Asked The Little Boy Who Cannot See' by Anon)

I asked the little boy who cannot see,
'And what is colour like?'

'Why, red,' said he,
'Is the colour of love, as beautiful as contentment,
The sweet smell of a delicate rose
And the colour of your blood from the sharp prick
Of its piercing thorn.

White is the crunchy white snow on a crisp winter morning
And the softness of a feather tickling the tips of my toes
To make me laugh and the viciousness of a snow leopard.

Brown is the warmness of a chocolate Labrador
Cuddling up to you with its slippery wet nose
And the taste of chocolate melting slowly in your mouth.'

Lauryn May Sturgess (11)
Cheslyn Hay Primary School, Walsall

I Asked The Boy Who Cannot See . . .

(Based on 'I Asked The Little Boy Who Cannot See' by Anon)

I asked the boy who cannot see,
'What is colour like?'
'Why, white,' said he,
'Is the softness of a feather,
And the low growl of a snow leopard
Prowling in deep white snow,
The smooth fur of a polar bear
Cautiously padding across the gentle fluffy ground.
Sparkling water from deep oceans
And stormy seas far away washing over my hands,
Ravenous rapids splashing on my soaked face, that is blue.
And red is the booming sound of flaring fireworks
Twizzling in the cool air,
The sweet scent of roses circling around my sensitive nose,
The furious fire of a smooth scaly dragon in the dark night.
Orange is the stalk of a tiger in the luscious forest foliage
And the juicy sweet taste of an orb-like orange.'

James Sturgess (11)
Cheslyn Hay Primary School, Walsall

I Asked The Little Boy Who Cannot See . . .

(Based on 'I Asked The Little Boy Who Cannot See' by Anon)

I asked the little boy who cannot see,
'And what is colour like?'

'Why, green,' said he,
'Is like a leaf, rough and wrinkled,
Spinning throughout the leafy forest.

Falling water, heavy like glistening snow
Landing on your tender hand, why that is blue.

And white is like a Siberian tiger,
Lovely, tender and warm,
And a gorgeous brush of soft fur over your hands.

And brown, is like a chocolate Labrador puppy,
Tender like chocolate melting on your pimpled tongue,
Also as soft as velvet.'

Reid Glaze (11)
Cheslyn Hay Primary School, Walsall

Me And Myself

I faff about with my hair every single day
Clips and bobbles flying in a special way.

My earrings are very pointy, especially at the top
When I squeeze them through my ears the pain never stops.

I love pets in every single way,
What a coincidence it makes at the end of the day.

I get lots of different friends every single day,
I get sad sometimes but sugar, spice and everything nice
Makes the glooms go away.

My cousins are so annoying but they can be helpful,
When it comes to family they're always there for me.

My teacher is Miss Leggett, she is so soft and sweet,
She smells like roses and that's such a treat.

My mom and dad are so caring and soft and sweet
They cuddle me up like a chocolate treat.

Paris Lauren Ramsay (7)
Cheslyn Hay Primary School, Walsall

I Asked The Boy Who Cannot See . . .

(Based on 'I Asked The Little Boy Who Cannot See' by Anon)

I asked the boy who cannot see,
'And what is colour like?'

'Why orange,' he said,
'Is the soft fur of a tiger, silky and soft,
And the sweet taste of an orange,
Juicy and sweet, tingling on my tongue.

And green is the aroma of freshly mowed grass
In a sweet meadow, swaying in the soft wind,
The chirping of a tiny grasshopper,
Hopping the day away.

Silver is the frost on a cold winter morning,
Freezing the world with the falling snow,
The silky softness of a snow leopard
Venturing the snow world.'

Zak Beebee (11)
Cheslyn Hay Primary School, Walsall

Spinning Round All Day!

There are many types of dancing,
Starting with ballet
But you need to learn to point your toes
And spin around all day!

The other moves of ballet,
Are chassé and jeté.
But the hardest one of all the moves,
Is spinning round all day!

The next type of dancing is tap,
Which is great.
You need to learn to shuffle ball change
And spin around all day!

The other moves of tap
Are shuffle, hop, ball change.
But first of all you need to learn
To spin around all day!

Isabelle Ellis (9)
Cheslyn Hay Primary School, Walsall

Colours

Red is a devil's gate
That drags in the death of people
Blue is a beautiful sky
Which is on a hot summer's day
Green is a dragon's spike
That points people when they get close
Pink is a heart
When somebody is in love
White is a cloud that floats nearby
When you are in a tall, tall mountain
Black is a cat
That sneaks by
Orange is the colour of an orange
Brown is a tank
That blows up in one flash
Yellow is the sun
That heats me up.

George Ellis (8)
Cheslyn Hay Primary School, Walsall

Hereford In Autumn

H olidays in Hereford
E arly morning mist
R iver flowing high, reflecting the sky
E verywhere orange and brown
F alling leaves twisting round
O pen fields all around
R apid river, rolling ripples
D iving ducks, graceful swans

I nvestigate forest fruit
N uts galore beneath fallen leaves

A utumn leaves seeming on fire
U p in the sky kestrels fly
T all trees naked now
U p in the night sky twinkling stars appear
M ilky Way very clear
N ow little creatures have a winter's sleep.

Daniel Cooper (9)
Cheslyn Hay Primary School, Walsall

My Friend Mario

If I could bring my friend Mario to school
I would learn him every rule.
Making a new friend
Is the beginning, not the end!
If you chat to them in class,
Your exams you will not pass!

Please don't shout,
That is definitely out.
Walk, don't run,
To get hurt is not fun!

Our teachers
Are not our preachers!
They can only guide us
If we work without a fuss.
Use their knowledge,
It could lead you into college.

Nathan Clarke (10)
Cheslyn Hay Primary School, Walsall

Boys, Boys, Boys!

Boys are always annoying,
My brother is rather strange,
He used to be annoying,
But now he's turned sweet,
Boys are always annoying,
Except my cousin Nat.

Nat is short for Nathaniel,
He is only a baby,
But he eats proper food,
I'm his favourite next to his mom,
I entertain him by dancing crazily.

I want peace and quiet,
Because it's really tiring,
To dance around
And listen to squeals,
What a hard life it is.

Halle-Mae Johnson (7)
Cheslyn Hay Primary School, Walsall

I Asked The Boy Who Cannot See . . .

(Based on 'I Asked The Little Boy Who Cannot See' by Anon)

I asked the boy who cannot see,
'And what is colour like?'

'Red is a huge dragon that flies as quick as a bat
The sound of his triumphant roar almost makes me deaf.
The feel of it makes a racing car go down my spine.

Green is sticky and minty like a hard boiled sweet,
It's as sticky as Velcro.

Yellow is as soft as a pillow, it's calm
And never loses its temper.

Black always loses its temper,
It's angry, mean and selfish.

Blue is wet and soothing like the sea,
It's the king of all colours.'

William Morris (10)
Cheslyn Hay Primary School, Walsall

The Old Lady

There once was an old lady
Who lived in a house
With mice and maggots
Coming out

She was never happy or glad
Always sad, sad, sad

Then one day she
Had a smack
On her head
And on her back

And from that day
She has never been
Sad or mean
Ever again.

Lewis Bullock (9)
Cheslyn Hay Primary School, Walsall

I Asked The Boy Who Cannot See . . .

(Based on 'I Asked The Little Boy Who Cannot See' by Anon)

I asked the little boy who cannot see,
'And what is colour like?'
'Why blue,' said he,
'Is the gushing water crashing up against the jagged rocks
On the shore as the tide comes in.

And black is the terrifying roar of an enormous puma
As it catches its prey and drags it ravenously into its cave
As the rocks hang down.

And red is a fiery, ferocious dragon
With orange burning hot flames bursting out of his mouth
Full of huge pointy teeth
As he hovers up to his gigantic rocky cave
As he tries to find some food in the dark night sky.'

Ben Leighton (10)
Cheslyn Hay Primary School, Walsall

I Asked The Boy Who Cannot See . . .
(Based on 'I Asked The Little Boy Who Cannot See' by Anon)

'What is colour like?'

'Why, red,' said he,'
'Red is a fierce, fiery, furious dragon
Flying over the colossal buildings so rapidly,
That it makes a racing car look slow.

Green is a plumped, juicy, ripe, gorgeous apple
That makes your taste buds dance and stand on end.

White is a soft pillow, gentle and smooth,
It's never frustrated, it's also frost on the trees,
The white crunches under your feet.

Blue is the calm water lying still hour upon hour,
That reflects and waits till someone touches it and sends ripples.'

Charlie Knobbs (10)
Cheslyn Hay Primary School, Walsall

Just Being Me

I want to be better at sports but I find it hard to kick a ball,
My legs don't do what I want them to and then I trip and fall,
I quite often bump into things, I just don't see them there,
And I promise I wasn't messing about when I fell off my chair.
I don't always understand what people mean when they talk to me
Or when I can't look in people's eyes they think I'm rude
But I don't mean to be.
People tell me to be more flexible, things aren't black and white,
But that's just confusing, I mean aren't things wrong or right?
I like to have routines,
I feel more comfortable knowing what happens in my day,
Changes really bother me, it stops me thinking about what I should,
I don't know what to say.
So my labels are dyspraxia and autism but they are a small part of me,
I hope people know I'm more than that and it's just Jack they see.

Jack Wood (9)
Cheslyn Hay Primary School, Walsall

My Grandma's Cat Dinky

Dinky is lazy,
Crazy,
Hazy,

When she's always daft,
Then she's last,
But I'm never glad,
When she's mad.

Dinky is cute only when she's happy,
But I'm never happy when she's wearing a nappy!

Dinky is lazy,
Crazy,
Hazy,

Sometimes she's bright when she bites.

Kyrsten Faith Clarke (8)
Cheslyn Hay Primary School, Walsall

I Asked The Boy Who Cannot See . . .

(Based on 'I Asked The Little Boy Who Cannot See' by Anon)

I asked the little boy who cannot see,
'And what is colour like?'

'Why, red is like a sour apple that sizzles on my tongue.
Oozing in my mouth like the *pop, bang, popping!* of a firework
Flaring in the dark midnight sky.
The soft feel of red remembrance poppies
That we wear in memory of those dear soldiers,' replied he.
'And, pink is the colour of little piglets
Rolling playfully in the sloppy mud.
The disgusting farmy smell lingering in my nostrils.
My lovely pink bouquet of roses sweetly scenting my room.
And white is like a stillness whilst you lie upon a cloud and dream.
The first fall of a snowflake melting on my tongue.'

Natasha Miller (10)
Cheslyn Hay Primary School, Walsall

Lovely Snow

Shiny snow glistened through the beautiful moonlight
That was gleaming like a crystal diamond,
Soft, tingly snow began to give me an abhorrent ache
Which made me freeze like a terrific snowman
Which had piercing eyes made out of silky buttons.
The charming snowman was like white fluffy clouds
Soaring through the calm, peaceful sky.

Freezing, frozen, fearful frost
Lay on the phenomenal grass like a sheet of glass.
Amazingly great cobwebs shimmered with delightful frost
Which made it sparkle like flaring fireworks
Shooting in the midnight sky.
Slowly gigantic icicles started to melt away,
And they were getting very diminutive!

Georgia Green-Howe (11)
Cheslyn Hay Primary School, Walsall

Football Players

F ootball players
O pportunity in front of goal
O pportunity from a penalty
T hat tackle was very bad
B ad foul again
A ttitude to the referee
L acking of speed
L osing the ball once again

P ossible to make the score 6-0
L acking of speed
A nd can't run anymore
Y oung talent on the bench
E njoyed because the manager's taken him off
R eferee, I'm really hurt.

Carter Platt (9)
Cheslyn Hay Primary School, Walsall

Mary The Fairy

There was a young girl named Mary
Who dreamed of being a fairy.
She danced around with a sparkly wand
And sat on a boulder near the duck pond.

Her glittery dress was as bright as a star
As was her tutu, tiara and car!
She really was a sight to behold,
Mary the fairy fast asleep on a cloud.

Her hair was as blonde as a shiny sun
And her nose was small and cute like a button,
Her lips fizzy pink from her earlier drink.

She really was a beautiful fairy,
That young girl, the dreamer, Mary.

Katie West (10)
Cheslyn Hay Primary School, Walsall

My Molly

My Milly Molly Moo,
She drinks water from the loo
And then she eats my grandad's shoe.

My Molly tries to steal my lolly
But I say no,
And then she bites my toe.

She waggles her tail like mad
And then she bites my dad.

When I put her food out
She likes to play about,
She likes to tip it out
And then she has a shout
And that is why I love my Milly Molly Moo!

Rosy Jane Carr (9)
Cheslyn Hay Primary School, Walsall

I Am The Drummer Boy!

I like to play my big black drum
Going *bang, bang, bang* all day
Mum says, 'Keep it down in there!'
'I've got to do my practice!' I say.

The music makes me feel good
Doing all my rhythms and beats
My favourite song is by Green Day
It gets me tapping my feet.

My drum set's got seven different things
There are two tom toms, a snare and a hi-hat
A crash, a low tom and a bass
I am the drummer boy and on the stool I sat

I played!

Alex Price (9)
Cheslyn Hay Primary School, Walsall

I Asked The Boy Who Cannot See . . .

(Based on 'I Asked The Little Boy Who Cannot See' by Anon)

I asked the boy who cannot see,
'What is colour like?'
'Why green,' he whispered,
'Green is like a wet soggy leaf
But pink smells like a blossoming rose,
Red is an upsetting poppy,
Blue, I hear is a running and rushing river
Falling down a waterfall as it goes,
And silver is cold, slippery, shiny ice on the ground
And white is freezing cold snow
And when you hold it
It feels like your hands are as hot as the burning hot sun
But now yellow is as bright as the sun.'

Natasha Smith (11)
Cheslyn Hay Primary School, Walsall

I Asked The Little Boy Who Cannot See . . .
(Based on 'I Asked The Little Boy Who Cannot See' by Anon)

I asked the little boy who cannot see,
'And what is colour like?'
'Why, blue,' said he,
'Is like blueberries on a plant, sweet and sour,
Snow leopards are as white as snow,
In the frost you can see their eyes glow.
And purple is like plums, sweet and sour
But incredibly tasty.
Yellow is the sun that beams down on your face,
Warming you up like it's a cold winter's day.
Light pink flowers must smell like perfume.
Red Nose Day, time to play and wear the squishy red noses all day
And green leaves dancing in the wind, full of excitement.'

Georgia Sanford (10)
Cheslyn Hay Primary School, Walsall

The Little Boy
(Based on 'I Asked The Little Boy Who Cannot See' by Anon)

I asked the little boy who cannot see,
'And what is colour like?'
'Why blue,' told he,
'It's the sound of trickling water spilling out the night sky,
Grass that is green, because green is the smell
Of luscious grass on top of the rocky mountains,
Orange is the heat beaming towards me just before nightfall,
Brown is the texture of the bark, squishing under my shoes,
Purple because it's the strong fragrance
Coming from the grasshopper field in the lavender countryside,
Red is the deafening sound of fireworks crackling
Across the pitch-black sky,
White is the snowflakes fluttering down to the soft white ground.'

Jack Williams (11)
Cheslyn Hay Primary School, Walsall

The Dragon

The dragon circled in the sky
Like a hawk.
The dragon circled in the sky
Like a helicopter
Only faster.
The dragon circled in the sky
Like a tornado
Only louder.
The dragon landed in his cave
Like a bird swooping into
A tree.
The dragon fell asleep
Like a bear
Going into hibernation.

Eve Rollinson (8)
Cheslyn Hay Primary School, Walsall

The Game

It's Sunday morning
We all line up
It's cold outside
We're playing for the cup.

Birchy and Flakey, what a pair
Playing up front, the crowd stare
Their quick pace and brill skills
They leave the defence standing still.

The whistle blows and it's away
They steady their nerves and begin to play
Josh and Jack playing in mid
George and Lucas at the back
That just leaves the keeper, his name is Zack.

Sam Birch (9)
Cheslyn Hay Primary School, Walsall

The Wonderful Thing About Monkeys

Monkeys are my favourite animals,
They're furry, they're cheeky, they're fun,
I like how they play in the sunshine,
They tumble, they gambol, they swing.

Their eyes are like shiny black marbles,
They smile, they sparkle, they stare,
Their fur is like sleek soft velvet,
It's soft, it's shiny, it's mad!

Monkeys should live in the jungle,
Be happy, be healthy, be free,
But the monkey I like most at the moment,
Is an old toy, is called Chimp,
And he's living at the foot of my bed!

Adam Lewis (10)
Cheslyn Hay Primary School, Walsall

My Garden

I run around the garden
And climb up a tree,
I hide inside the bushes where nobody can see.

I hike up my mountain,
I swim in the sea,
I wish that everybody could join me.

I run in the jungle,
I push a boulder down,
But nobody will ever see me in my dressing gown.

I climb down my mountain
And push down the tree,
Tomorrow hopefully you can meet me.

Ella Rose Proverbs (9)
Cheslyn Hay Primary School, Walsall

Garden Poem

In the garden there are many different things that you can see.
Like bluebells, roses and if you're lucky you might see a golden fox.
The lawn is crisp in the summer but it is wet and soggy in the winter.
The beautiful sweet petals of a daisy smell
Like a bumblebee's fresh honey from his hive.
There are lots of noises in the bright sunny garden,
If you listen hard you can hear them all.
Like the buzzing of a bee, or the wind chimes
As they gently bang and crash together in the soft air.
Or see the merry children play on the toys that they are given.
The birds come to eat the delicious nuts that have been put out for them.
Look at the baby birds fly, but they will soon be gone
When they have grown, perhaps they will return next year.

Kate Ordidge (10)
Cheslyn Hay Primary School, Walsall

Talking Chickens

I have five hens,
Mostly white, brown and black,
They write with pens
And sleep in a sack.

They play silly games all day long,
Having fun with a different name,
After breakfast they sing a song,
Then fly off in their own little plane.

I feed them veg and fruit and corn,
Which they have enjoyed since the day they were born,
You can hear them clucking all day and night,
You know to own a chicken is just so right.

Ben Smith (9)
Cheslyn Hay Primary School, Walsall

Dirty Daisy

There once was a girl named Daisy,
Who always wore a ripped dress.
She had the dirtiest hair on the planet
And was always in the biggest mess.

Her packed lunch was a disaster,
And so was her dirty tea.
Her family were the messiest,
The messiest as can be!

Daisy owned a clean cow,
As clean as clean could be,
The cow was called Clean Colin,
Daisy thought, *it's just like me!*

Harriet Slym (9)
Cheslyn Hay Primary School, Walsall

A Special Treat

It increases my waist
But oh what a taste

Creamy and delightful
Heavenly and blissful

Smooth and sweet
A scrumptious treat

Velvet and milky
And so very silky

A mouth-watering smell like no other
But what can it be?
Tasty delicious chocolate for me. *Mmmm!*

Thomas Greensill (10)
Cheslyn Hay Primary School, Walsall

Friends

Friends are important when you start school
They make you happy when others are cruel
Sometimes you're happy and sometimes you're sad
When I play with my friends I always feel glad
Some friends are boys and some friends are girls
Some friends have straight hair and some have curls
Some are tall and some are short
Some like lessons and some like sport
Boys like football and girls like to run
At school I like skipping, it is such fun
Your friends will stay with you from junior to high
At the end of the day my friends will say bye.

Abbie Yates (10)
Cheslyn Hay Primary School, Walsall

I Asked The Boy Who Could Not See . . .

(Based on 'I Asked The Little Boy Who Cannot See' by Anon)

I asked the boy who could not see,
'What do colours mean to you?'

He said that, 'Red is the sign for help or danger,
Blue is like the ice in my drink,
Yellow is the sun; bright and happy,
Silver is the frost glimmering and gleaming,
Pink is the candyfloss at the summer fair
And gold is friendship; solid and true,

Now what do the colours mean to you?'

Abby Carr (10)
Cheslyn Hay Primary School, Walsall

I Asked The Boy Who Cannot See . . .

(Based on 'I Asked The Little Boy Who Cannot See' by Anon)

I asked the boy who cannot see,
'What is colour like?'

'Green, is like hopping frogs that hide from you and me,
Blue is the lake water running downstream like a marathon,
Yellow is the wonderful feeling when the bright sun rises,
Red are the poppies blooming from the waterfall of heartbreak,
White, the empty mind, and the fluffy drifting clouds,
That are like candyfloss,
And silver is the sparkling moonlight when you look out your window.'

Chloe Hildreth (10)
Cheslyn Hay Primary School, Walsall

Rubber Duck

R ubber duck goes quack
U gly duckling turns into a swan
B ubblebath for the ducks
B ursting bubbles as they swim
E very duck needs some love
R ubber dub, dub.

D ull life for the ducks
U nder the water bobbing up and down
C urling around and around the plughole
K eep me company in the bath.

Savannah Till (9)
Cheslyn Hay Primary School, Walsall

I See Dogs

I see dogs,
One blurry, one furry,
One bigger than a lake,
The floppy ears,
The big furry tummy,
The nice biscuits too.

George Bicknell (7)
Cheslyn Hay Primary School, Walsall

I Asked The Little Boy Who Could Not See ...
(Based on 'I Asked The Little Boy Who Cannot See' by Anon)

I asked the little boy who could not see what is colour like?
'Well,' he said in a sweet sounding voice, 'this is what it's like . . .
Red must be the colour that says stop,
Blue is the colour of the sky,
Green must be the colour of grass;
Spiky and cold as it waves goodbye,
Pink is the sweet smell of summer that travels through the sky,
Yellow must be a butterfly that flies from flower to flower,
White must be snow that softly falls down to the ground.'

Joseph Hughes (10)
Cheslyn Hay Primary School, Walsall

The Loving Cup Of Tea

Get the tea bag in the beautiful cup,
Boil the water for the one you want.
Pour the milk
And stir it around.
Add a sweet spoon of sugar
And the best of your heart.
Try three cups of love
And stir it about.
It's the one cup of tea no one can spare,
It's the love they need.

Harriot Donnelly (8)
Cheslyn Hay Primary School, Walsall

Chocolate Poem

Chocolate, chocolate, chocolate, chocolate, chocolate,
When you take a bite, you will taste its delight!
Chocolate, chocolate, chocolate, chocolate, chocolate,
It is so nice, sometimes covered in rice!

Chocolate, chocolate, chocolate, chocolate, chocolate,
It will make you scream and sometimes will be covered in cream!
Chocolate, chocolate, chocolate, chocolate, chocolate,
When you take a nibble at the side, it will take you on a fantastic ride!

Sam Gadd (10)
Cheslyn Hay Primary School, Walsall

Red

Red is for the Devil's favourite demon
Or for a red-hot chilli
Or a fire-breathing dragon.
Red is for a sports car, Buggati Veyron
Or a hot air balloon
In the crystal-blue sky
Or the red-hot sun.
Red is for a big clown nose
Or flaming fire.
Red is for the Champions League ball.

Cameron Osborne (8)
Cheslyn Hay Primary School, Walsall

Colour Poem

Light blue is the colour of the sky,
That birds sing way up high,
When you pass the bright blue sky,
You hear people passing by,
Light blue is the colour of a happy day
With the sun shining every way,
Blue is the colour of the sea,
All the fish looking at me,
When you pass it you can smile as much as you want
Because you love it, you are part of one.

Lily Jordan (8)
Cheslyn Hay Primary School, Walsall

Football

F ootball is the best, it's amazing
O n the ball once again
O n your head me son
T ime ref, I'm hurt
B all comes to you, what ya gonna do?
A t a penalty where's it gonna go?
L osing again lads, this is not good
L ads I've changed my mind because we got one back.

Thomas John Taylor (9)
Cheslyn Hay Primary School, Walsall

I Asked The Boy Who Cannot See . . .
(Based on 'I Asked The Little Boy Who Cannot See' by Anon)

I asked the boy who cannot see,
'What is colour like?'
'Green is a sweet apple tingling away at your tongue,
White is like the soft, smooth snow covering your frozen feet,
Yellow is the colour of the burning sun heating up your body,
Red is the colour that represents the English soldiers that fought in WWII,
Orange is a juicy, sour orange fresh from the shops,
Purple is the colour of the dangerous thunderstorms.'

Regan Smith (10)
Cheslyn Hay Primary School, Walsall

The Rainbow

Red is the colour of roses
It's also the colour of noses on a cold and frosty day
Orange is the colour of a sunset slipping behind the calm blue sea
Yellow is the colour of a bright sunflower gazing over me
Green is the colour of dew-covered grass on a fresh spring day
Blue is the colour of a cold blue sky
Indigo is the colour of a deep, dark cave
Violet is the colour of a tiny flower peeping shyly by the stream.

Jack Hughes (8)
Cheslyn Hay Primary School, Walsall

School

School, I like it, not all the time.
You stand by the office if you do a crime.
The best lesson is PE,
It's better than playing on the Wii.
At playtime you get to eat and play
But it's a pity it doesn't last all day.
Sometimes we do fun things
And we rush home when the bell rings.

Max Wheeler (9)
Cheslyn Hay Primary School, Walsall

The Rat

Once I saw a rat,
It was a little bit fat,
But when I looked into its eyes,
I got a little surprise,
Its eyes were the colour
Of the sun about to rise!

Ben Colgrave (9)
Cheslyn Hay Primary School, Walsall

Teacher, Teacher

Teacher, teacher,
You need a rest,
Only because you're
Always the best.

Teacher, teacher,
Come here quick,
I need help,
I cut my lip.

Teacher, teacher,
No more school!
Let's go to town
And look so cool!

Teacher, teacher,
Let's go home,
It's time for us
To roam.

Simran Kaur & Pavindeep Kaur (10)
Devonshire Junior School, Smethwick

Birthday Wishes From My Mum

Dear sweet, sweet daughter
I love two things
One is a rose and you
The rose is for one day
And you for ever, ever, ever.

Gursimran Kaur Sapra (8)
Devonshire Junior School, Smethwick

Chocolate

   C is for caramel, *mmm*
   H is for hazelnut, *mmm*
   O is for orange, *mmm*
   C is for Cadbury, *mmm*
   O is for Oreos, *mmm*
   L is for Lindt, *mmm*
   A is for Aero, *mmm*
   T is for Twix, *mmm*
   E is for eclair, *mmm*

What does it spell?
Chocolate!
All of the yummy chocolates
In my tummy, *mmm!*

Arneet Uppal (8)
Devonshire Junior School, Smethwick

Bees

   B ees give us honey.
     Mmmm!
   E at up all the honey.
     Mmmm!
   E at all the honey, bees love honey.
     Mmmm!
   S it at the table and eat all the honey.
     Mmmm!

What does it make?
It makes bees!

Gagandeep Singh Josan (7)
Devonshire Junior School, Smethwick

Ed

Ed, Ed, always wears red
He has a dog that hasn't been fed
He spends all day in bed
Ed, Ed, loves chocolate spread.

Davina Kaur Dhatt (8)
Devonshire Junior School, Smethwick

Romans

Romans, Romans,
Are so clever.

Romans, Romans,
Can build a wall.

Romans, Romans,
Are so strong.

Romans, Romans,
Are so strange.

Simranjit Kaur (7)
Devonshire Junior School, Smethwick

Happy

H is for high
A is for, 'Argh!'
P is for plant
P is for play
Y is for yay!

Guess what is it?
Happy!
Happy is about having fun!

Arundeep Kaur Dosanjh (7)
Devonshire Junior School, Smethwick

Spiders

Spiders, spiders
I hate spiders
I wish that I could squash them
And I could tread on them.
Eeek!

Elliemay Simcox (7)
Devonshire Junior School, Smethwick

Romans

Romans, Romans
Came to England
Built a lot of walls
Oh! Romans, Romans
They love to take control.

Summer Strode (7)
Devonshire Junior School, Smethwick

The Person I Like The Most

The person I like the most
Is probably my mom when she makes me toast

Or maybe my dad, oh he is great
But when he eats, he makes a state

Or maybe my brother, oh he is funny
Yet embarrasses me when he dresses like a bunny

Or maybe Mr Hall, oh he is cool
Yet again he is a fool

The person I like the most
Doesn't lie or boast

The person's name begins with an L
And always has great stories to tell.

Thomas Belcher & Liam Felton
Hall Green Primary School, West Bromwich

Love

L onely and you find a soulmate
O pened up hearts
V alentine's Day I depend on
E motional gifts like chocolates.

Iyesha Young (11)
Hall Green Primary School, West Bromwich

The Great Fire Of London

The Great Fire of London - a major blaze,
Incredibly lasting over two days.

From the heart of the town to narrow alleys,
The death toll rose high on the tally.

It spread like a virus through old cobbled streets,
Praying for rain or even sleet.

The Thames offered water and escape by boat,
But people found it quicker to swim or float.

Dangerously dark in the cold, bitter winter,
Wooden houses burnt down to a cinder.

The Great Fire of London - a major blaze!

Bethany Perry (10)
Hall Green Primary School, West Bromwich

Titanic

Titanic was a large boat,
I'm amazed it could even float.
Many, many people died,
Watching the film people cried.
The icy waters hit like a knife,
People fell in and lost their life.
On that horrible, nasty, cold night
People died - it was a fright.
On that day night came upon,
The ship cracked in half
And then it was gone.

Shannon Rachel (10)
Hall Green Primary School, West Bromwich

Five Terrible Tigers

Five terrible tigers on a sunny day.
Five terrible tigers prance and play.
Five terrible tigers eat and eat, night and day.
Five terrible tigers we can see no more.

Jack Hayward (9)
Harden Primary School, Walsall

Dance, Peacock, Dance

Dance, peacock, dance,
Make the rain come.
Dance, peacock, dance,
Banish the sun.

Dance, peacock, dance,
Beat on the drum.
Try, peacock, try,
To make the rain come.

Charlotte Bellingham (8)
Harden Primary School, Walsall

Elephant

I love elephants
Elephants love me
Elephants think I'm nice and cute
I think they are too
They love peanuts, oh so much
I love peanuts too
They are so crunchy
I love elephants.

Holly Hall (7)
Harden Primary School, Walsall

Elephant

E njoy the sun
L ong trunk
E ars that flap
P lodding slowly
H eavy steps
A mazing size
N ice knees and toes
T iny tail.

Kadie Johnson (7)
Harden Primary School, Walsall

Elephant In The Zoo

There was an elephant sitting in a tree,
Eating lots of leaves
And drinking mugs of tea.
I said to my mom,
'What shall we do?'
She said, 'Shut up and run
And get out of the zoo!'

Charlie Fellows (8)
Harden Primary School, Walsall

Peacock

P leasing colours
E yes of blue
A stounding bird of India
C learly loved by all
O ne-eyed feathers
C ommon in India
K een to display their colours.

Tilly Mansell (8)
Harden Primary School, Walsall

Pleasing Peacock

P leasing colours
E yes of blue
A mazing display
C lever and witty
O utstanding colours
C heerful and bright
K now they are beautiful.

Hadia Rohail (7)
Harden Primary School, Walsall

Tigers Have . . .

A terrible roar.
Its nose is brown
And it's got grand looking stripes.
Exciting to see.
Rare and special.
That's the tiger.

Sophie Middleton (8)
Harden Primary School, Walsall

Twelve Terrible Tigers

Twelve terrible tigers on a spring day
Twelve terrible tigers crawl and play
Twelve terrible tigers have a treat each day
Twelve terrible tigers we can see no more
Each in a den they will stay
Till they are bigger and hunt away.

Hamza Rohail (9)
Harden Primary School, Walsall

Tigers

The claws are as sharp as a knife,
Tigers are special,
That's a tiger!
Tigers are exciting to see,
They live in the jungle,
Tigers are dangerous.

Matthew Foster (7)
Harden Primary School, Walsall

My Tummy (About A Tiger)

My tummy is furry
I like it like that
I wiggle around
I jiggle around
My tummy is furry.

Courtney Hall (9)
Harden Primary School, Walsall

Tiger

T eeth made for biting
I t lives in the jungle
G reat claws
E xciting to see
R eally special, that's a tiger.

Natasha Westley (7)
Harden Primary School, Walsall

Three Lives Of God

Hope shoots through my beautiful windows which read a holy story
Colours sparkling in every direction, dancing like a gorgeous monkey
Amazing carvings are rubbed in every direction
Of my surrounding proud walls
Huge stone musclemen carry my handsome ceiling
Who gives God my magnificent call.
Millions of pews are filled and polished
With the humble souls of loving people
My welcoming charming entrance
Conceals a magical world which is always faithful
Enormous, huge and magnificent I may be but inside the baby cross,
Hope is waiting to jump out.

Demolished, destroyed and punched right through.
Burnt into evil nasty ashes
I'm just a useless skeleton now
Mountains of rubble are climbed by naughty dancing flames
Crumbling stone walls fall over and die in seconds
All my hope and love is sucked up with an enormous vacuum
But the tiny cross still stands proud, watching all the chaos
God is still on my side

I'm a whole new beauty, all cleaned up
Bursting full with exciting tourists
Laughing happily with my friend at my side
There's not a spot where excitement doesn't lie
Bombs are extinct
They don't even dare to blink
The phoenix is rising out of the ashes
Coventry Cathedral is alive.

Nishant Rai (11)
King Henry VIII Preparatory School, Coventry

A Dragon's World

At last her search was over, her life was now decaying away,
She knew he was gone forever, but why, no one would say,
Surrounded by the cold, black rock where she lay.

Now she lay dying and defeated, drowning in her own tears,
Knowing she could go no further, wanting an end to her fears,
While she remembered her loved ones and dears.

She cried out in anger to the lord of dragons to ask him why,
Why had the golden dragon left her, and let love pass her by,
And let her lie here and die.

From far away the great lord of the dragons heard her cry,
And with a great roar like a lion he swooped down from the sky.
He also made sure it was not a lie,
That made the beautiful princess cry.

This magnificent lord, king of the dragons, in his supreme age,
Born of the wind, fire and water, and now filled with deadly rage,
But the fire within is trapped in a cage.

He saw the tears on the face of this beautiful dying princess,
The roaring fire became dwindling and instead his heart filled with tenderness.

He vowed to banish the golden dragon who had done this thing,
To give her back her life again, make her smile, laugh and sing.

He would take her back to his castle and care for her until then,
But he knew that if he did this, he would never let her go again.

She opened her eyes and saw him, and the love showing on his face,
Then she knew she would live again, and for her there was a place,
He wanted to murder the golden dragon with a mace.

He had promised her a journey to somewhere far, to find her dreams,
And safe in the knowledge he loved her, discovered what hope means,

He promised her a journey to somewhere far, to find her dreams,
And safe in the knowledge he loved her, discovered what hope means,

He promised her the gargoyles and fairies, and with a wave of his hand
Removed forever from the silver dragon, the power he had to command,
After all, all this was his land.

So the silver lady will once more be loved and cared for, safe all her life
The lord of twelve dragons will never hurt her with a knife,
Maybe one day she will be his wife.

Darshan Parekh (11)
King Henry VIII Preparatory School, Coventry

Blitz Poem

Raging sound of the siren
Banging in my head
People charging to reach the nearest shelter
My mother drags me with all the others
The stinky smelling gas mask covering my face
My little sister crying like a baby

Suddenly a loud thud!
A bomb
As the bombs got louder
My heart got louder
If I held my fears in any longer
I would burst out crying
Children crying
Children wailing
Bombs exploding
My heart racing
Finally the all clear

I held Mother's hand tightly
Slowly, steadily
I stepped out
A city in flames
Mountains of rubble
Disheartened
Speechless
Abandoned
Choking smells
Why?
Is this a dream?

Simran Banga (10)
King Henry VIII Preparatory School, Coventry

A Monster Of An Adventure

The sea was silent.
The air was still.
All was calm.
Then alarm bells rang.
Sudden swift dark shadows passed under the boat.
Ripples turned into waves
As the sea got angry.
Thwack!
The boat lifted in the air
Like an exploding water fountain.
Men screamed
As the ship was thrown down
Crashing back into the sea.

A monster reared up and out
Its underbelly covered in
Savage scars so deep
You could climb up them.
Its eyes like fire
Alight with anger.
A strangled, deathly silence.
Then it came crashing down.
Crunch!
Masts tore.
Swords shattered.
The ship split in two.
'Abandon ship!'
The cries of sailors
As they flew off deck.
Silence . . .
No survivors except for
One lonesome sailor
Floating into another adventure . . .

Matthew Pandya (9)
King Henry VIII Preparatory School, Coventry

Evacuee Poem

My family have left me behind in the country
They are back at home, at least I am safe now
I will miss them so much
I have left tall buildings, the noise
Some of my friends are at home
That have not been evacuated
All the traffic I am leaving, all the shops

I am an evacuee, you can tell by the look of me
With a gas mask around my neck
And shoes which look a wreck
With a teacher by my side
I feel more petrified

I am staring out of my window
All I can see are puffs of steam
Acres and acres of land right in front of me
I am petrified of these strange animals
It has never been sunny ever in London
There is a farm in the distance which I can see

I am an evacuee, you can tell by the look of me
With a gas mask around my neck
And shoes which look a wreck
With a teacher by my side
I feel more petrified

When I got off the train I stood in line
This mean man came over
'That young girl will do,' he said
I stepped forward, it was terrifying
He told me to hurry up, he was an old strict man
Moody, I am going to have to be well-behaved with him.

Georgina Peake (10)
King Henry VIII Preparatory School, Coventry

My Most Favourite Things

I have a bunch of favourite things,
Some I do not show.
I keep them safely hidden,
In a place they do not know.

Half of them are soft toys,
I'm a fan of those cuddly things.
My favourite is my monkey,
On to me it clings.

Another is my DS,
I have a hundred games.
My favourite is 'Picture Master',
Where you have to design frames.

I love my board games too,
I have the most popular ones.
My favourite is 'Minefield',
Where you have to catch the guns.

I also love to read,
I have the best-selling books.
One of them so scary,
Since he is surrounded by hooks.

I collect a lot of key tags,
None of them the same.
Though my favourite is the 'N',
As it stands for my name.

My most favourite thing of all,
Is of course my secret box.
This is where I keep my most precious thing,
With about two hundred locks!

Nuwanji Amarasekera (11)
King Henry VIII Preparatory School, Coventry

An Evacuee's Inventory

This is my vest,
This is my nightie
And these are my stockings,
With their woollen strands dangling limply.

My mask,
Lying in its brown box,
The mask, it turns me into a monster,
The smell, oh, the smell unbearable.

My label,
Tied to my neck,
Treating me like a parcel,
Sent away from home.

Here is my teddy,
Staying by me always,
A memento of my 5th birthday,
Always there to comfort me.

Here is my locket,
With a picture
Of my mummy and daddy,
Never leaving my neck.

Here is my blanky,
Always in my view,
With a beautiful flower,
Sown on by my mummy's smooth hands.

This is my silver thruppence
Pressed into my hands,
By my kind daddy,
This wishes me luck, in the darkest of times.

Elisabeth List (10)
King Henry VIII Preparatory School, Coventry

Blitz Poem

Sitting, listening to crackled music,
The radio
When a wail, the air raid siren, starts
We stampede to rusty shelter
For our lives, we climb in
Like monkeys in the wild
With the siren still screaming
Like a newborn.

In a shelter I cower from overhead spitting of guns
As the air raid begins
With babies screaming in unison with the siren
Playing cards scratching the tables
A whizz, a boom and I know they got next door
And probably my house too!
Whizz, bang, they got the butcher's
Fear fills my head
Children wail like banshees.

Next morning, 'All-clear!' crackles across the radio
Relief soothes my mind
I clamber out of the shelter
When shock gains control
As I look onto my street
Horror fills my heart
As in front of me are piles of bricks
That I used to call my home
So I search through bricks
And cry.

James O'Leary (11)
King Henry VIII Preparatory School, Coventry

Calm Sea, Heavy Sea

Wild waves crashing angrily
Slimy, scaly seaweed swirling softly
Silver, slippy fish calmly swimming
Nippy crabs fastly scuttling around
Sandy, rough water freezing madly
Frothy, white foam whirling side to side.

Rebecca Aspinall (8)
King Henry VIII Preparatory School, Coventry

Evacuee Poem

Mum, Dad and Grandma standing at the door.
Crying, praying that I won't get hurt.
I beg not to leave home, I just can't.
I am going to miss my bedroom, my house and even the city.
The evacuee form has been sent.
I'm definitely leaving today.

I'm an evacuee.
You can tell by the look of me.
With a gas mask around my neck,
Shoes which look a wreck.

I sit on the train,
I wait to feel my pain.
I hear the train, louder as it speeds up.
I see the city leaving, as we approach the valley.
I feel scared, nervous; I could go on all day.
I just don't know who I'll meet today.

I'm an evacuee.
You can tell by the look of me.
With a gas mask around my neck,
Shoes which look a wreck.

We've arrived at the countryside, the sun shines and the grass grows.
We're all frightened to death; we're all in a mess.
It's selection time, everyone's standing in line.
Oh no! It's Mrs Brick, tough and as hard as a hammer.
Where will she take me? What will she think of me?
Oh Lord, please help me get through this terrible time.

Abbie Smith (10)
King Henry VIII Preparatory School, Coventry

The Beast From The East

Washed up carcass lying on the dry sand.
Sparkling white fangs as sharp as a sword's blade.
Giant jaws snarling.
Mucky brown horns standing straight.
Skin rotting yellow.
Black eyes as dark as the midnight sky.

Harrison Waugh-Smith (8)
King Henry VIII Preparatory School, Coventry

Inventory Of An Evacuee

Here I am about to depart and at my side is . . .

My gas mask
Placed in its boring brown cardboard box
This is my label so limp and dull
Because of that everyone would treat me like a parcel.

My soap is white and plain
But I'm not to complain
My night attire
As soft as feathers in a beautiful powdered blue.

Soft like clouds
Is my vest with a lamb stitched on the chest.
My knickers I'm proud of most
White with beautiful blue frills.

My gold locket
It glistens and shimmers in the light.
My precious pound
Pressed in my hand as the train sets off.

My lime-coloured notebook
Will be waiting when I'm bored
The secrets I have discovered
Will be hidden inside it for evermore.

My exquisite fountain pen
Will lie in its pale blue box
Which I chose in a daring midnight-blue
This is my inventory, can you write yours?

Anais Dosanj (10)
King Henry VIII Preparatory School, Coventry

The Dangerous Sea

Wild, conquering waves crashing dangerously,
White, frothy foam flying high in the sky,
Vast, rushing water whirling dangerously,
Heavy, slippy rocks, showing just above the water,
Giant, quick, silvery fish jumping high out of the water,
Salty, stinging water spray flying into my eyes.

Sam Duckers (8)
King Henry VIII Preparatory School, Coventry

The Bombs

Panic, screams,
Shoving to safety.
Screeching siren
Popping ear drums.
Out of tune cat orchestra.
A noise you can hear in the USA,
Annoying everyone as it plays.

Panic, screams,
Pushing, shoving,
Down to darkness.
Bruises covered with dirt,
Scrum for a bunker,
Who wants a bunker?
Cold metal frame,
Lice infested, stinky mattress,
Plus a boy on top of you who loves to jump.
Boom!
Soot fell from the ceiling.
Silence fell.

Crying, sorrow
In an organised form.
Floods of people appear from trenches,
Holes in roads, half houses
Seeing skeletons of buildings,
Smell of ash, gushing water
The war strikes again.

Laura McTernan (11)
King Henry VIII Preparatory School, Coventry

War Poem

Crash! Bang! Smash!
Bombs dropping from the sky.
Landing on the floor with a bang!
Crash! Bang! Smash!
Children crying as bombs destroy houses.
Lives lost very quickly.
Faster than a plane.

Aaron Hayre (10)
King Henry VIII Preparatory School, Coventry

The War Station

He held on to his mother,
He saw the train coming near.
He said goodbye beneath his breath,
He started to shed a tear.
He held on to his mother,
He saw the train coming near.
He was worried for his safety,
He felt his veins touch fear.
He was an evacuee.

She held on to her little son,
She saw the train coming nigh.
She tried to put on a false smile,
She hid her tears up high.
She held on to her little son,
She saw the train coming nigh.
She cuddled him without regret,
She looked, eye to eye.
She was a mother.

He saw the train arriving,
She wept a bigger flood.
He cut himself on his box,
She wiped away the blood.
He jumped on the filling train,
She had to shout goodbye,
He waved back with his little hand,
Oh why? Oh why? Oh why?

Jacob Knyspel (10)
King Henry VIII Preparatory School, Coventry

Mufasa Poem

Royal Mufasa standing tall and proud
Strong powerful Mufasa watching his pride
Soft, smooth mane drawing round his head like a golden crown
Sharp, strong teeth cutting through a piece of meat like knives
Shining claws shimmering like swords
Shimmering eyes as black as midnight
Brown fur covering him like golden silk.

Asmaa Ahmad (9)
King Henry VIII Preparatory School, Coventry

Timon And Pumba

I know a warthog
He is as heavy as a bulldozer
With a tufty black tail
That's Pumba!

I know a meerkat
He is as mad as a monkey
Who is completely insane
That's Timon!

They're both irrepressible
As lively as a firework
They're very likeable
That's them!

I know a warthog
With big nostrils flaring
He has yellow eyeballs
That's Pumba!

I know a meerkat
He's a bad comedian
And as lively as a loose spring
That's Timon!

They're always enthusiastic
They're light-hearted
And they're joyful animals
That's them!

Esha Joshi (9)
King Henry VIII Preparatory School, Coventry

Kingfisher Flight

Kingfisher flight,
Landing on branches in the river.
Catching fish in beads of light,
Kingfisher flight,
Waiting patiently.
Landing when you might,
Kingfisher flight,
You gave me a fright!

Sophie Oliver (10)
King Henry VIII Preparatory School, Coventry

Timon And Pumba

Fat Pumba has one big bushy tail
Chubby Pumba is as heavy as a bulldozer
Pumba's sharp yellow tusks defend his life
That's Pumba!

Insane Timon is as lively as a firework
Hyperactive Timon makes a bad comedian
Crazy Timon sometimes can be annoying
That's Timon!

Adventurous light-hearted Timon and Pumba squabble a lot
Enthusiastic Timon and Pumba are unusual sometimes
The dynamic duo are inseparable like Ant and Dec
That's them!

Pumba's warty, lumpy face has luminous yellow eyes
Greedy Pumba is always hungry
Pumba's big nostrils flare open as wide as a tunnel
That's Pumba!

Potty Timon goes completely bonkers
The mad meerkat is as light as a feather
Berserk Timon is as nervy as a deer
That's Timon!

Timon and Pumba are as close as peas in a pod
Energetic Timon and Pumba are as daft as a baboon
The troublesome twosome, Timon and Pumba, can be stupid
That's them!

Jordan Parker (8)
King Henry VIII Preparatory School, Coventry

Red

Red is for an embarrassed teenager trying not to cry,
Red is for remembrance when we think of people that have died.
Red is like a blushing rose which has fallen from above,
Red is for a chilli roasting in the glistening sun.
Red is for a ruby which stands out from a crowd of glittering jewels,
And red is definitely a colour not fit for any kind of fool.
It's just like a king, all rich and strong,
But all it wants to say is that you're never on your own.

Emriece Heer (11)
King Henry VIII Preparatory School, Coventry

Pumba And Timon

He's as fat as a bus
From eating a shed load of bugs
One yellow tooth in his massive jaw
That's Pumba!

Fizzying around like a spark
He's as lively as a spring
A large personality for a small creature
That's Timon!

Inseparable like Jedward
But always squabbling too
They are like happy brothers
That's them!

Tufty black tail swinging in the breeze
Chubby belly swaying as he runs
Croaky voice like a toad
That's Pumba!

Telling loads of terrible jokes
He seems as daft as a brush
You don't know what he'll do next
That's Timon!

They will always stick together
Like jolly peas in a pod
Whatever they do they are never dull
That's them!

Oliver Kenyon (9)
King Henry VIII Preparatory School, Coventry

The Flowing Sea

Magical water that is swirling by the warm calm wind.
Wild angry waves moving up, down, up, down slowly.
Fluffy frothing froth slipping, slip, slop, slip, slop beautifully.
Smooth, sparkling pebbles plopping, dropping.
Slimy, slippery seaweed flowing under the sea.
Gold, cute, shiny fish swimming gently.
The reflection shines out above the sea.
What a gentle calm sea!

Vedika Bedi (8)
King Henry VIII Preparatory School, Coventry

Dynamic Duo

As ugly as a lumpy lizard,
As smelly as a stinkbug,
With stubby legs, chubby belly and a wobbly voice,
That's Pumba!

As funny as a chunky monkey,
Lively as a cheeky chipmunk,
He speeds like a cheetah with skinny legs and insane voice,
That's Timon!

As inseparable as salt and pepper,
They work together like day and night,
Squabbling, quarrelling but always cheerful,
That's them!

Heavy as a pile of pineapples,
Fatter than a hairy hippo,
With sharp yellow eyes and a tufty black tail,
That's Pumba!

As lively as baby baboons on a boat,
As funny as a giggling gazelle,
Crazy like a fizzy firework, bad joke teller,
That's Timon!

As adventurous as aardvarks,
Enthusiastic as energetic entertainers,
Irrepressible and friendly they're the good guys,
That's them!

Anastasia Jeffcoat (8)
King Henry VIII Preparatory School, Coventry

The War Is Taking Over

You hear the bangs,
The sirens, the crowd.
You know the war is coming.

You look out the window,
Bombs are falling, people crying.
Nazis taking over, nobody is brave.

The war is coming, silently, silently.

Bethany Isard (10)
King Henry VIII Preparatory School, Coventry

Timon And Pumba

Pumba is as ugly as a frog.
He is fatter than an elephant
And as heavy as a bulldozer.
That's Pumba!

Timon is crazier than a chipmunk.
He is as nervy as a deer
And as funny as Mr McGrane.
That's Timon!

They're the dynamic duo.
They're inseparable like Ant and Dec
And are very likeable.
That's them!

Pumba has bright yellow eyeballs.
He has big nostrils flaring
And has sharp yellow tusks.
That's Pumba!

Timon is as lively as a firework.
He is a very bad comedian
And is as light as a feather.
That's Timon!

They're very good guys.
They're always enthusiastic
And they're light-hearted.
That's them!

Deepinder Singh Dyal (9)
King Henry VIII Preparatory School, Coventry

The Mean Deb Monster

Eyes were red as blood.
Horrible skin like abandoned food.
Sharp fangs like razor blades.
Ears like leathery bat wings.
Dark empty eyes like an open grave.
Shrunken skin rough as sharp rocks.
Where will it go next?

Caitlin Newport (9)
King Henry VIII Preparatory School, Coventry

Timon And Pumba

As heavy as a bulldozer with fat stubby legs.
Fatter than a panda bear with a big chubby belly.
As ugly as a hyena with a big yellow blunt tooth.
That's Pumba.

As lively as a firework and sometimes annoying.
A bad joke teller and a bad comedian.
As funny as Mr McGrane and completely insane.
That's Timon.

The dynamic duo are inseparable like Ant and Dec.
They are adventurous and annoying.
They're enthusiastic and happy, joyful and cheerful.
That's them.

He has a warty, lumpy face with sharp yellow tusks.
He has big nostrils flaring and a tufty black tail.
He has big bold yellow eyeballs.
That's Pumba.

As crazy as a monkey going mad.
As fast as a cheetah running around.
As nervy as a deer and as lively as a loose spring.
That's Timon.

They are light-hearted and always there for Simba.
They are very friendly creatures.
They sometimes squabble over silly things.
That's them.

Alexandria Quinn (9)
King Henry VIII Preparatory School, Coventry

The Monster Of The Deep

Sharp fangs like razor blades biting viciously
Jet-black eyes glaring aggressively
Fierce fin resting on his head
Skull lying there silently
Jaws open wide and threateningly
Ears like bats' wings flapping in the breeze
Beware the monster of the deep!

William Astle (8)
King Henry VIII Preparatory School, Coventry

Pumba And Timon

Fatter than a hippo,
Wider than the Nile,
Heavier than a tank,
That's Pumba.

Funnier than Michael McIntyre,
As nervy as a deer,
Jumpy like a kangaroo,
That's Timon.

Inseparable like Dick and Dom,
Stuck like glue,
The dynamic duo,
That's them.

Chubby belly swinging to and fro,
Stubby legs and yellow tusks,
As warty as a toad,
That's Pumba.

Crazier than a hyena,
With jokes worse than Mr Brown,
I'm sure and I'm certain he's completely insane,
That's Timon.

Enthusiastic duo,
Bright as fireworks,
Always friendly and joyful,
That's them.

Abigail Forsythe (8)
King Henry VIII Preparatory School, Coventry

The Evil Head

Fierce head lying in the wet sand
Skull-white fangs as sharp as elephants' tusks
Curbing towards the sky
Black eyes as black as midnight
With terrifying pupils glowing brightly
Old wrinkly skin as rotten as old food that reeked
Huge jaw opening like a cave with massive muscles.

Toby Barham (8)
King Henry VIII Preparatory School, Coventry

Evacuee

I didn't want to leave my family,
But we all had to flee,
I stood there in a crowd of sad people,
Their tears treacle,
I looked around scared as could be,
I gave my mum and dad a big plea,
I didn't want to be on my own,
I gave a big groan.

My dad opened his arms,
I went over and touched his palms,
He lifted me up and squeezed me tight,
With all of his might,
Then he pulled me down and my mum pulled me up
As quickly as she could,
She definitely knew she should,
She whispered into my ear, 'Be a brave boy,'
She gave me my favourite toy.

I got put down on the floor,
I wanted more,
I now felt alone,
I really wanted it to be postponed,
Tears dripped down my face as I sat down,
I didn't want to leave the town,
I knew they didn't want to leave me,
But I was now an evacuee.

Emma McCabe (11)
King Henry VIII Preparatory School, Coventry

The Blitz

Sadness crawls through the land,
German bombers attacking in their deadly bands,
Bang, bang, down it goes,
The cathedral roof in one go.

Wreckage covers the broken city,
Death's song ringing in people's ears,
How will it be rebuilt?
This broken city gone up in flames.

Matthew Leatherdale (10)
King Henry VIII Preparatory School, Coventry

Bombs

The siren starts whining
A piercing scream
Like a cat when you step on its tail
People don't laugh
They're in a state of panic
Pitter-patter, pitter-patter
The sound of racing feet.

People in their shelters
The shelter of dread
People crying, waiting for bombs
There's silence, a whine
Then *bang*
Like an earthquake
Bang
Silence

The whirring starts again
People wander out of shelters
Gasping of shock
Houses destroyed, demolished
Devastation everywhere
Fiery infernos
Rubble, ash, smoke all around
A smell of death and smoke
My house, gone
Is this Coventry?

George Wilkinson (11)
King Henry VIII Preparatory School, Coventry

Sirens

Stunning sirens singing quietly
High cliff rumbling slowly
Enchanting song hypnotising beautifully
Shiny ship sailing smoothly.

Beautiful sirens transforming wickedly
Screeching sound piercing sharply
Deserted beach swallowing madly
Ancient bones rattling crazily.

Dhruv Parekh (8)
King Henry VIII Preparatory School, Coventry

The Evacuee

I have all my things packed
My gas mask pounding against my chest
My label flapping in the wind
Dreading the months ahead of me
A new place
New people
I'm scared

I have my bodice in my bag
Just one to keep me warm
Two pairs of stockings to keep my feet snug
These things are needed

All these things remind me of home
The sights, the smells, the sound, how they feel
Holding my teddy so tightly
Hearing the jingle of my locket

Just sitting here now reading a letter
Sent to me by my mother written with great care
My blanket just next to me, all folded neatly
Stitched by my father with great pleasure

Then finally, my shoes polished so they shine
To play in the garden all day long
I also have a comb to do my hair
To make it so neat
When will it end?

Mary Gittens (10)
King Henry VIII Preparatory School, Coventry

Giraffe Poem

The giraffe's tail swishing from side to side beating the flies.

The tall legs running energetically towards the swaying trees,
The giraffe's tail swishing from side to side beating the flies.

The long neck taking the huge pink tongue to the leaves,
The tall legs running energetically towards the swaying trees,
The giraffe's tail swishing from side to side beating the flies.

Karsha Dosanjh (9)
King Henry VIII Preparatory School, Coventry

The Vampnake

The vampnake,
The vampnake,
His favourite food is chips and steak!
He's got a dying, dripping top!
His curly hair sticks up in locks.
His mouth could house a hive of bees
And he's still screaming from the hot tea.
He screams,
Argh.
Hooot.
His arms are shaped like a crab.
He rocks.
He's sad.
The vampnake,
The vampnake,
He loves licking chocolate cake.
Last night he crawled up a drainpipe
And ate a grape (which was ripe).
He is tall, wide and is sly.
He creeps up at eight o'clock
So beware children don't stay up long.
He chews.
He slithers goo.
He lollops.
The rest is mostly gulps and gallops.

Anisha Gill-Saluja (10)
King Henry VIII Preparatory School, Coventry

Mufasa Poem

Sharp claws like fangs biting.
Skilful feet as fast as a car.
A body as tough as an elephant.
Close looking eyes staring suspiciously.
Razor teeth like piercing daggers.
Long thin whiskers like mice tails.
Powerful legs as strong as metal.
Vibrant tail like a kite in the sky.
Walking elegantly like the king.

Havandeep Khatkar (9)
King Henry VIII Preparatory School, Coventry

The Bombers

There it was, the dreaded sound,
Ringing and screeching in my ears.
It had started.
People running frantically around me.
I retreated into the safety of the air raid shelter.
I was safe, for now.
Scared, frightened, anxious,
So many feelings all at once.

Nothing to do but listen and wait.
Sounds of bombs getting louder and louder.
Whizz, whizz, bang over and over.
Fear masked the faces of the people around me.
The fear of death.
Minutes seemed like hours and hours seemed like days.
Eventually silence.
It was over.

Injured people stumbling out of the shelters.
Shocked and confused.
I looked for familiar surroundings
But every inch of land was destroyed.
Smoke and ash engulfed me.
Rubble as tall as mountains lay everywhere
Crushing the people who lay underneath it.
When would it end? When would it end?

Sanjeet Chhokar (10)
King Henry VIII Preparatory School, Coventry

The Lion Poem

The sleepy lion lying on a rock.

Razor-sharp claws shining wonderfully
On the sleepy lion lying on a rock.

Brown mane blowing in the wind
With razor-sharp claws shining wonderfully
On the sleepy lion lying on a rock.

Lauren Cox (9)
King Henry VIII Preparatory School, Coventry

Inventory Of An Evacuee

I've got my coat
My great winter coat,
That comforts me
And keeps me warm.

My brown box:
My plate, my mug,
Into my box
I've wrote my name.

Wrote it with
My blunt pencil,
Which I keep hidden
From the noisy.

My teddy bear
Makes me feel safe
When I'm sleeping.
It's too precious
And that makes it priceless.

I carry a notebook
To write a diary of
My life but guess
I don't need it because
I'm staying in a
Rich man's house.

Jordan Gumbura (11)
King Henry VIII Preparatory School, Coventry

My Giraffe Poem

The tall giraffe chomping slowly.

Her long tail swishing gently in the breeze
As the tall giraffe was chomping slowly.

Her glittering eyes shone brightly
As her long tail swished gently in the breeze
While the tall giraffe chomped slowly.

Jacqueline Correa (8)
King Henry VIII Preparatory School, Coventry

Inventory Of An Evacuee

The train departs,
Steam puffs out,
The whistle blows,
We're moving.

My heavy suitcase,
Packed to the brim,
With socks, vests, soft toys and all,
Left by my side.

My name tag,
Tied tightly around my neck,
It gives me the sensation,
That I'm a parcel.

Handkerchiefs,
Photos,
Footwear and money,
These are all things that comfort me.

But most precious of all,
Is the thing in the box,
Which I show,
To no one.

I'm safe,
For now.

Visva Moorthy (11)
King Henry VIII Preparatory School, Coventry

Mufasa

Royal Mufasa standing tall and proud
Loving Mufasa licking his cubs
Fearless Mufasa protecting his pride
Strong Mufasa watching his pride like an eagle
Long, smooth mane crowning him as a golden crown
Angry Mufasa roaring at his brother
Kind Mufasa sharing his land
Elegant Mufasa smiling as he should
Brave Mufasa risking his life
Nice Mufasa helping his son.

William Kelly (9)
King Henry VIII Preparatory School, Coventry

The Slavinog

The slavinog,
The slavinog,
Its breath looks just like bright green fog!
Its skin is thin and made of tin!
Its tentacles suck from within!
Its voice is weirdly strange and high,
And funnyish,
Bellowish,
Sly!
Its blood is purple and bumpy,
And thumpy,
And lumpy,
Jumpy!
The slavinog,
The slavinog!
Last night it gulped down Anne, my dog!
As you are there having your bath!
It will slither down your garden path!
I advise you now to make your will,
Cos now it's here, ready to kill.
You loll,
It contemplates,
It lollops,
The rest is merely gulps and gollops.

Chelsey Johnson (10)
King Henry VIII Preparatory School, Coventry

My Dead House

I walked outside in front of my house.
I can't call it home, it's a ruined dead house.
Pictures burnt to the ground, frames smashed.
My memory vanished because of all the heat of the fire.

I'm in the shop, not harmed at all.
Buy some clothes and some food,
Maybe a book or magazine.
I'm going on a train, don't know where but somewhere.
Hopefully somewhere where it is lovely, cosy
And a nice place.

Lewis Mohindra (10)
King Henry VIII Preparatory School, Coventry

The Kraken

The aroma of the salty seawater
Filled the air.
The ship rocked gently
On the calm salt sea.
When suddenly . . .
Bang!
A long, slimy, jade-green tentacle
Reaches out
Like a tree pulling from its roots.
The tentacle
Wraps itself around the weak bodies of the sailors.
Shouting,
Screaming,
Begging for mercy.
A terrible roar ran through the air.
Guns exploding
And the tentacle cuts through the boat
Like a knife.
Clinking of metal,
Screaming of men,
Roaring of wind.
Bang!
And *t*hen,
Silence . . .

Maariyah Sulaimaan (10)
King Henry VIII Preparatory School, Coventry

Red

The sly red fox creeps around town,
Going up hills and coming down,
He sneaks into a small alleyway,
Wondering what he will find to play,
But all he saw was the sky,
Shining brightly like red dye,
He wanders down to a stream,
Where the water faintly gleams,
Then he strolls back to his den,
Via Farmer Bill's chicken pen.

Hannah Lucy Allen (11)
King Henry VIII Preparatory School, Coventry

The Pegafish

The pegafish,
The pegafish!
Its eyes are red and devilish!
Its hair is long and slimyish!
Its breath kills and is smellyish!
Its fangs are rank and rottenish!
And greeny,
Slimy,
Leathery,
Its tail is fat and rubbery
And sucky,
Smelly,
Blubbery!
The pegafish!
The pegafish!
I sat it at half-past twoish!
Last night it was with some big fish;
Tonight it's in a dirty dish!
As you are in your cosy bed,
It drags up its heavy big head,
You scream,
It roars,
You yell,
Your teddy bear is all alone.

Josephine Kunc (9)
King Henry VIII Preparatory School, Coventry

Blue

As calm as the sea
As blue as the sky
As tasty as a blueberry
Blue is everywhere
As relaxed as a cat
As quiet as a mouse
As blue as a snowflake
As blue as frost
Blue like an icicle
Blue is always there on a winter's day.

Amelia Moore (10)
King Henry VIII Preparatory School, Coventry

Blitzed

The siren wails.
Everyone rushes in the pitch-black, midnight moon.
Pushing and shoving, clueless, mindless.
You couldn't see where to go.
Just a dim light.

Inside the air raid shelter
Sounds of screams and parents protecting their children,
By holding their hands,
Boom, bang, crackle,
Giant bombs aim and hit.
The ground above shakes and trembles.
Dust falls.
Everybody puts their gas masks on.
They all look like monsters.
As the roof shatters and cracks.

We walk outside, anxious, worried.
Some people say, 'Are we still in Britain?'
As families gather round the rubble
And hunt for their houses.
The smelly, stinky smoke fills the air.
Houses
Demolished.
Blown up.

Lyle Sargent (11)
King Henry VIII Preparatory School, Coventry

Yellow

It is autumn today
with the yellow leaves falling off the trees
getting ready for winter.
Yellow bananas sat in the fruit bowl
waiting to be touched by life.
In the streets the children play,
laughing and joking all through the day
in the hot yellow sun, yes the children play.
The yellow is gone, the white is here
but yellow time will be back next year.

Matthew Ratcliff (10)
King Henry VIII Preparatory School, Coventry

Inventory

I've got my book,
My pencil case
And my money.

A pack of sweets,
My food, my snack,
In its packet.

A can of eggs,
My plate, my mug,
Into its tin
I've scratched my name.

My carry case holds
My pyjamas
And a couple of things.

This is my book
And this is my quill,
This is my wooden sock,
This is my cap.

The quill's the thing
I love the most,
By day it writes stories
I make up at night.

Karam Singh Budwal (11)
King Henry VIII Preparatory School, Coventry

The Deadly Sea Monster

Higher and higher the waves are towering,
Crashing, tumbling and foaming as they land.
The angry clouds thunder down with rain lashing into the sea.

Deadly tentacles slithering faster and faster
He attacks!
Crushing, killing, devouring beastly monster.

The waves calm down.
The sea is blood red.
The monster drifts away slowly, contently.
The deadly sea monster sleeps away!

Nayan Kyle Mistry (9)
King Henry VIII Preparatory School, Coventry

The Life Of An Evacuee

I'm staring through my window,
As frightened as a little fly,
Hoping those hours stay on standby.
Packing my bags, who knows how long for?
Belongings and memories spread out on the floor.
Going to the station feeling so sad,
Can't bear to say goodbye to Mum and Dad.
On the train feeling alone,
Longing and longing desperate to go home.
A new family comes; I feel upset,
They'll never replace the family I've left.

No more free seats, guess I'll just have to stand,
I wish, for one last time I could hold my mum's hand.
My memories are slowly fading away,
I want them, I need them to stay.
Where am I going? Is this a dream?
Out of the window, why can I see grey, dirty steam?
Butterflies flutter in my stomach, feeling shy,
For some reason I'm excited, I don't know why.
I'm split in half, with mixed emotions.

This is the life of me,
When I was an evacuee.

Ria Sanghera (10)
King Henry VIII Preparatory School, Coventry

Lion Poem

The majestic king roaring in the jungle.

The golden mane like rays of sunshine
On the majestic king roaring in the jungle.

The razor-sharp teeth glinting like the stars
With the golden mane like rays of sunshine
On the majestic king roaring in the jungle.

The rumbling hungry belly accompanies
The razor-sharp teeth glinting like the stars
With the golden mane like rays of sunshine
On the majestic king roaring in the jungle.

Holly Slack (9)
King Henry VIII Preparatory School, Coventry

The Kraken

The Kraken, the Kraken, the sharp wind whispered,
As the ship slapped something hard and bony,
The clang of the bell rose in curious pursuit,
Sailors swung round in fright and panic.

Unexpectedly water transformed, dark and gloomy,
A piercing shriek was let out from below,
Suddenly the ship was showered in spray,
A khaki tentacle lifted blubbery, warty, putrid.

Sailors screamed like the battle alarm,
Clanging of metal heard miles around,
All hands grabbed at swords and spears,
Thrashing and stabbing for their lives!

The wind whipped the sailors' wounded faces,
Slimy tentacles rose up from the deep,
Mast collapsed like an uprooted tree,
Splintering, shattering, splitting and snapping!

Ship cracked catastrophically,
Tentacles dragged souls to their watery grave,
Ship gave one last gasp slipping silently into the deep,
In terror one and all tumbled into the murky ocean,
Silence.

Louisa Rowlands (10)
King Henry VIII Preparatory School, Coventry

The Lion's Eyes

The walnut-like eyes looking cautiously.

Long mane swaying gently in the breeze,
Like a collar around the proud face,
With walnut-like eyes looking cautiously.

Giant paws quietly slapping the ground
As the lion slowly approaches its prey,
His long mane swaying gently in the breeze,
Like a collar around the proud face,
With walnut-like eyes looking cautiously.

Kai Wayne-Wynne (9)
King Henry VIII Preparatory School, Coventry

The Minoton

The Minoton!
The Minoton!
So tall that it blocks out the sun!
Its toenails are quite disgusting!
Its so old skin is rusting!
It's boldy,
Mouldy
And crazy,
It's bulbously wild
And lazy!

The Minoton!
The Minoton!
Last time it demolished my mum!
Yesterday it snored in Chile;
Now under my brother Billy!
As you brush out your tangled hair,
It breathes out dark red putrid air,
You brush,
It breathes,
It smackers,
Now,
It *attackers*!

Ellena Marlow (9)
King Henry VIII Preparatory School, Coventry

Mufasa

Angry Mufasa roaring fiercely
Handsome Mufasa standing tall and proud
With his golden mane drawing around his face.
Mufasa has elegant, silky, long brown fur.
Strong powerful teeth like thorns in his mouth waiting for its prey.
His eyes scanning for any enemies on his way, like agent cameras.
Loving Mufasa licking his cub.
Alert ears listening carefully.
Brave Mufasa fighting aggressively, like a big brown bear.
Jealous Mufasa staring at his brother.
His claws so sharp, he could tear his prey apart.
Black eyes as midnight skies.

Imaan Turudi (9)
King Henry VIII Preparatory School, Coventry

The Kraken

Waves crashing
Warning bells ring
One man swung overboard
Sailors shrieking,
'The Kraken, the Kraken, the Kraken.'
Mucous, glutinous tentacles rising
From the blue salty seawater.

Guns advancing
Axes hacking
Revolting slime
Sails fracturing
Howls of mercy.

Splinters piercing the guiltless pirates
Males being swung around
Tentacles rising from the deep
Slithering up the side of the bateau
Its feelers crushing the boat to smithereens.

Retreating in silence the vicious beast pleased with itself
Returning to its master the monster vanished
The crackling of the fire the only sound on the sea
No survivors left, everything demolished.

Ravi Parekh (10)
King Henry VIII Preparatory School, Coventry

Sea Poem

Waves whirled wildly like a whirlpool.
Waves crashed viciously like a tornado.
The sea bashed monstrously like an elephant.
The surf rocked wildly side to side.
The waves dribbled all over the place like a hurricane.
The tide came in outrageously.
The water ridges were larger than life.
The ocean was so deep like a bottomless pit.
The sea animals drawn into dawn into the dark.
The waves gushed towards the sands.
The sea swished like a goldfish.
The sea erupted like a firework, loud and high.

Ria Patel (9)
King Henry VIII Preparatory School, Coventry

Blitz

'Come on, Sir,'
Tripping over the heavily scattered rubble,
The unidentified man ushered me
Into a small sandbag surrounded room.

Crash! Bang!
Fear lurked in everyone's soul,
Sweat trickled down people's foreheads
Due to the boiling temperatures.
Children clutched tightly onto their toys,
Mothers clutched tightly onto their children.
The room now looked smaller,
The smell of burning crimson flames wafted up my nose.

As the last bomb fell,
People gave a sigh of relief.
Parents wandered out while
Huddling close to their children.
Mouths dropped to an O shape,
As they saw their homes destroyed.

Even though times were tough,
People thanked God
That they were still alive.

Simran Dhugga (10)
King Henry VIII Preparatory School, Coventry

The Kraken

The bursting stormy wind was shouting.
The dark sea jolted across.
As the sea roared like a bear,
The creaky, wooden boat crashed.
There was silence no more.
The Kraken suddenly appeared
To devour you.
His slithery tentacles crossed the boat.
His arms were ready to throw you.
He killed everybody except one man.
Before you knew it he disappeared
Into the depths of the sea.

Daniel Mirfendereski (10)
King Henry VIII Preparatory School, Coventry

Evacuee

The train was arriving, I felt terrible
Leaving my mum and dad was the worst thing that could ever happen.
I missed my older brother and my older sister
Who were living with my parents in this miserable war.
I couldn't believe my eyes because I'd have left my unforgettable toys
And my cuddly, soft teddy bear.
Look at the fields, they are awfully bombed and wrecked.
To me it feels like I am leaving my friends, my toys, especially my parents,
My brother and sister and the beautiful home.
I see a farm with all the weird animals that I don't know.
I see a war plane drifting past like a rocket.
I see the black, foggy smoke puffing.
I see houses far away that are blown up.
I see black objects gliding in the blue, bright sky.
I see half burnt trees nearly collapsing to the ground.
The train was stopping in the rusty old station.
I walked out of the train and was offered some chocolate cake.
I was forced to stand in front of the wall.
I waited impatiently for someone to choose me.
I saw two kind people wanting to have me.
They took me through the dark tunnel
And away to somewhere I didn't know.

Maadesh Raveendran (11)
King Henry VIII Preparatory School, Coventry

The Stormy Sea

The stormy sea raging rapidly across and over the village
And all the boats around it like a herd of charging elephants.

Thunder and lightning cracking and flashing
In front of your very eyes
As hurricanes and tornadoes gurgle and thrash the sea
Like an over stirred cup of tea.

The terrible waves are like man-eating monsters
And they could probably gobble you up in one small bite.

I bet the sea could defeat you with pleasure and delight
As you can probably see you can never defeat the sea
And its mighty strife.

Rachel Carron (9)
King Henry VIII Preparatory School, Coventry

War Poem

My mum kisses me goodbye,
As she wraps me up.
She puts my coat, scarf, gloves and hat on,
While my dad packs my bag.

As I left my dad handed me my bag,
And put my name tag on.
I ran outside as I saw my friend,
I could see her through the letter box.

I shouted to my mum and dad,
'I love you,' and blew a kiss.
I started to walk backwards,
Till my parents were out of sight.

When I got to the station,
I sat next to my friend.
We were so excited to go to England,
The time went so quick.

There was an old lady,
Who came round with chocolate.
So of course she gave us some,
She said we were so cute she gave us extra.

Kyra Jayde Jones (10)
King Henry VIII Preparatory School, Coventry

Blue

Calm like a pond in the middle of the grass the blazer,
Lies on the bed peacefully with his best friend Jumper,
Then he looks out of the window to see,
The very blue sky above the very blue sea.
Everything in the room is calm and peaceful,
Then the relaxed scene is spoilt by Mr Bluebottle.
The blue top and the blue jeans,
Are stacked up nicely like dictionaries.
The blue ink spilt on the white paper,
Is spreading out like some sort of danger.
Then the blazer goes to sleep,
Like his pet mouse, called Peep.

Priya Bains (10)
King Henry VIII Preparatory School, Coventry

Inventory Of An Evacuee

My pillow made of steel,
My coat made of wool.
This is my wooden suitcase
Filled with boring clothes.

I've got a packet of penny chews,
For the train journey of quite a few.
I have my brown worn out bear,
So I won't trouble.

I have two cotton cream socks,
So I won't get cold.
My tattered scarf wrapped around my neck
To keep me warm.

This is my hat,
Knitted by my mum.
I have a little charm with me for good luck,
Who am I going to stay with?
God knows.

I have a lovely mother who loves me very much,
Don't let me go,
I miss her already!

Zahra Mushtaq (10)
King Henry VIII Preparatory School, Coventry

Evacuation

Woolly socks with my cap,
Goes with my ragged clothes,
My dress is dirty.

My favourite pair of black shoes,
With a buckle going across.
I buckle my shoes and do up my coat,
What a day this will be!

Wrapped up warm, that's what I like to be.
Walking down the street with my mum,
Tightly squeezing her hand,
Hopefully noticing how much I love her and . . .

Maisie Jane Taylor (11)
King Henry VIII Preparatory School, Coventry

Journey To The Unknown

I look behind me, at Mum and Dad,
A bit scared, but really sad.
By myself, and all alone,
Hoping that one day, I can come home.
Clutching my teddy, oh so tight,
I hate the war; I don't think it's right.

I grasp the rail, climbing on the train,
When I get there it won't be the same.
I hope they're nice, my new carers,
I hope they're good, as good as parents.
I open the window, freeing my hair,
I've never smelt the countryside air.

It's not so bad, now I'm here,
I haven't dropped a single tear.
I was first one picked; they said I look nice,
And for dinner we had chicken and rice!
I like it here, in the country,
Then even have an apple and a pear tree!

And that's the end, the end of my story,
I now live here with pride and glory.

Esmé Dublin (10)
King Henry VIII Preparatory School, Coventry

The Kraken

It swirls the ship and surrounds,
The ship rocks back and forth like a baby in a cot.
A stench like fish food disperses through the air,
As its tentacles rise through the waves,
Like a swarm of bees.
It's th-the Kraken!
It suffocates then lollops pirates,
With its rubbery but robust tentacles.
Grasping them down to the icy sea,
It takes them for a nasty bite.
Guns fire bullets,
Men stumble like injured cheetahs,
But all is too late.

Ishita Jainer (9)
King Henry VIII Preparatory School, Coventry

Air Raid

Piercing sound through the city.
Air raid siren seeking to be heard.
Hopeless people hurrying towards steel shelters.
I took one last look at my home, frightened, terrified.
Will everything still be there?
Will anyone die?

Everyone huddled in the shelter,
Sitting with anticipation in the stone-cold bed.
Planes roaming the air above dropping bombs.
Choking smoke filling the air.
Was it my home?
The whistle screeched into our ear to give us the all-clear.

Everyone huddled to the door.
I could hear people crying with devastation.
Finally I got my first glance of the city.
I walked through the rubble.
I walked and walked because there was nowhere to go.
I sat on the rubble of my home,
Hopeless,
Alone.

Caitlin Roper (11)
King Henry VIII Preparatory School, Coventry

The Stormy Sea

The stormy sea crashes against the slippy rocks.
The stormy sea rages out of control at the shore.
Lightning lights up the bay at night.

The stormy sea gushes powerfully like a wizard.
The stormy sea collides together against the lighthouse.

The rain pours down violently on the shore.
All the shells in the sea wash away into another place.
The next day all the rocks are slippy and wet
And all of the people's houses are flooded.

The sea is now calm and gentle.
The seagulls cry as they glide.
Searching for food after a stormy night.

Harriet Morris (9)
King Henry VIII Preparatory School, Coventry

Kraken

The black clouds rise in the air.
The sea roars like a lion.
It rains heavily.
Lightning comes.
Misty.

The Kraken.
The slimy, slithery tentacles race up the boat.
Its teeth are as sharp as blades sticking up at you.
It crunches the bones of a shark.
All the other sharks hide in fear of the Kraken!
Even a great white shark.
The deadly sea monster, the Kraken.
Its eyes are wide,
Staring at you.
Its shin as hard as sticky skin.
Its breath as smelly as old cheese.
It can hear you from a mile away.

Once the Kraken has killed them all,
He swims away
Calmly.

Rahul Nayyar (10)
King Henry VIII Preparatory School, Coventry

The Creaker

Clouds swirling in the air
Water bubbling like it is boiling
The thunder is shouting across the sea
Boat is rocking from side to side

The monster is throwing people into its mouth
The monster curling its tentacles around the boat
People screaming like a load of girls
The suckers are glue

The monster goes but no one knows where he goes
The screaming has gone
Apart from the monster
Roaring its way back to the deep where no one goes.

Harriet Rayner (9)
King Henry VIII Preparatory School, Coventry

The Thing

The ship was sailing
Navigating the vast sea
The thunder was roaring with rage
The rain was hammering down
Like there was no tomorrow
The crew were terrified
Of the dangers that lay ahead

In the far distance ahead
A mammoth imposter ship approached
At the front of the boat
Flapping wings as big as an elephant's ears
Was a ghastly, ghostly, gigantic gold ghoul
It flew and swooped on the sailing ship
There was a smell of death in the air
Not a member of the crew survived

The sailing ship sank deep, deep, deep down
It rested at the bottom of the sea and now the crew's souls float
In the depths of the gloomy sea
Their job is to protect other sailors
From the danger of the ghastly ghoul!

William Walker (9)
King Henry VIII Preparatory School, Coventry

Into The Inferno

Into the inferno I go,
Not knowing where to throw,
The buckets from the Fow,
Will get this fire out you know.

Clang, clang, the bells go,
To the engines, hurry, hurry,
Get to that hangar, that one there,
A big bellowing plume of smoke.

Will we all survive
Or will some not come out alive?
I really hope I stay alive,
Through this fire we go.

James Trigger (10)
King Henry VIII Preparatory School, Coventry

Why, Oh Why, Is It Me?

With children standing all around me,
All looking confused.
At least I'm not on my own, oh no!
It's not just me; they are coming with me!
Mum looks worried and frightened,
But I don't know why,
Why oh why, is she getting upset over me going on holiday
As she had told me before?
Maybe she was jealous, but there's something else,
What oh what, is it?

Again, she looked at me with her ashen face,
As if she didn't know me!
Mother hugged me like I was leaving forever,
And spoke one word, 'Goodbye.'
'Where am I going?' I finally asked.
My mother answered in her crying voice,
All I could understand was, 'You are an evacuee,'
I was an evacuee, what's that?
Steam rose all over the station, as the train pulled up.
I'm an evacuee!

Tom Lees (11)
King Henry VIII Preparatory School, Coventry

Under The Sea

Down below under the sea,
A creature lives,
Who nobody's seen,
He sleeps by night
And hunts by day,
He was woken up by the roar of the thunderous storm,
He climbs up the boat with his slithery tentacles,
Rocking the boat from side to side,
Knocking and crashing,
The boat into pieces,
He eats the people,
With his teeth as sharp as swords
And lets the boat sink to his home,
Under the sea.

Jay Jassi (9)
King Henry VIII Preparatory School, Coventry

A Stormy Day

The stormy sea crashed against the bay
Very, very far away.
And it crashed and it bashed like a big pile of rocks.
As the lightning lit up the sky.

The big tidal wave swept up all of the crabs,
And all of the other sea animals.
It thrashed onto the flat surface of the sea,
That was calm and gentle.

The lightning struck when the sea swirled violently.
The lightning zig-zagged across the sky instantly.

The whirlpool whipped around violently with a violent fury,
Like a tiger jumping around madly.
It bashed the little wooden boats about,
That were floating on the sea.

The pieces of the smashed up boats
Were jumping up in the air like a salmon.

The powerful sea towered like mountain peaks
For the final time.

Ellinor Smith (8)
King Henry VIII Preparatory School, Coventry

The Kraken

Tentacles covered with lethal suckers.
Colossal suckers climbing up the side of the slippery boat.
Terrified men snatching their weapons.
Harpoon guns being blasted at the great creature.
Screaming people being hurled overboard!
Sailors have goo fiercely spat at them.
The taste of goo in their mouth.
Splinters in their hands.
Huge tentacle rises out of the shimmering water.
Drops down onto the powerless men.
Cracking the boat,
Turning it into splinters . . .
Silence.
Apart from the waves crashing against each other!

Samuel McLeod (9)
King Henry VIII Preparatory School, Coventry

The Squidafly!

The squidafly!
The squidafly!
One red, ferocious, glaring eye!
Tentacles, all long and scaly,
His diet is ten children daily!
His head is big and balloony,
And sometimes he goes very loony!
His squelchy suckers, slimy too,
And out of them, there's lots of goo!
The squidafly!
The squidafly!
His teeth are as blue as the sky!
Last night it lurked inside my bed,
Tonight it will be in your shed!
As you are shouting, 'Squidafly!'
He flies all over the sky.
You scream.
No one hears you.
He gets closer.
No one is going to save you . . .

Keerat Dhadda (9)
King Henry VIII Preparatory School, Coventry

The Storm Monster

The black sky,
The black sky.
Sea crashing,
Thunders roaring like a lion.
Rising from the dark sea,
A black eyed monster,
Tentacles slithering up the side of the boat,
Smash!
Voices screaming,
No
And help.

Gulp,
Gulp,
The monster returns to the bottom of the sea!

Aum Sharda (9)
King Henry VIII Preparatory School, Coventry

An Evacuee

I am an evacuee
Lonely I walked to the black train.
I took one more look at the wonderful city.
You would see the odd glance of the plane.
You would be missing a magnificent thing.
You would be leaving it forever.

I am an evacuee
When I was on the train I saw these big black things.
I could see the train's steam gliding past the window.
The clicking and clacking eventually took me to sleep.
I woke because of the tooting of the train.
The train shook like a bull tossing a stack of hay around.

I am an evacuee
I was as nervous as a dog meeting its owner.
My knees were like shattered glasses.
My head was ringing with children going past the door.
I was the only one left.
Then an old man pointed at me in disgrace.
He looked at me in astonishment.

Alex McLean (10)
King Henry VIII Preparatory School, Coventry

My Eyes

What my eyes have seen:
They have seen the bodies after the Blitz,
The mounds of the dead,
Crumbled houses with people still in them.

What my eyes have seen:
They have seen the dead in battle,
The wounded by the guns,
Craters with piles of dead filling them.

What my eyes have seen:
They have seen the burning planes falling from the sky,
Anti-air guns shooting down planes all night long,
How the push of a button can kill hundreds
And they don't even see their victims.

Matthew Small (11)
King Henry VIII Preparatory School, Coventry

The Kraken!

Stench of seawater
Sails flapping in the ferocious wind
Bells ringing
Water as cold as ice
Bubbles
Grasping tentacles rise up the rotting wood
Slithering around the mast
Grabbing
Clanking metal-like spears
Panting like a dog
Wrapping like vines
Screaming
Screeching
A mournful cry
Bursts like an erupting volcano
Bang!
Crash!
Snap!
Gone.

Michelle Panteli (10)
King Henry VIII Preparatory School, Coventry

Stormy Sea

Slimy seaweed slowly comes into view.
Angry whirlpools out of control smashing shells ashore.
Lightning strikes, lighting up the sky.
Watch towers watch for anything bad nearby.
Huge waves are angry like tsunamis as big as mountains.
Lightning lights the sky like massive lanterns.
Glowing scales of fish lighting up the sea.
Just like glow worms in our back garden, go and see.

Divers diving down for treasure.
But all they find are boxes of leather.
Birds roaming the sky.
Lightning falling in the blink of an eye.
Boat being battered by brutal waves.
No land within miles.
Will their lives be saved?

George Gawthorpe (9)
King Henry VIII Preparatory School, Coventry

Blitz Poem

The sound of the siren
Played back in my brain,
Excruciatingly painful.
Eeeeeeeelaaaae.
Red and black crosses scattered in pitch-black sky.
Everybody rushing to shelters.

I lay on a seat,
A cup of cold tea, German bombers drop deadly loads.
Lights shudder, screaming bombs,
Just a fraction of what was to come.

The second siren screamed,
I pushed my way through crowds
And couldn't believe my eyes.
Tangled wires,
Cracked, destroyed buildings,
Long thin cables.
I rushed to my house, petrified.
My house - my home obliterated.

Amun Sangha (10)
King Henry VIII Preparatory School, Coventry

Evacuee

I stepped on the train, it felt really weird,
I had never been on a train before.
I felt lonely sitting on a cloth seat, in the carriage.
I didn't know who I would meet today.
The train started to go,
I was leaving the city behind me.
I see the city, then I looked again, there were trees and grass.
Someone walked up to me, offered me bread and a drink,
Then I refused it.

I stood in a line against the wall looking cool.
Gas mask on my left, bag on my right.
Standing up to be picked.
Lots of people went, not me.
I was the last waiting for a parent.
Mr Mean was there, he looked mean.

Emma Lawrence (11)
King Henry VIII Preparatory School, Coventry

Evacuee

I'm an evacuee, why did it have to be?
Crying myself to sleep.
People think I am a contrary child
And I try not to be.
I have a cold coat and uncommon uniform.
Why me?

Farms go by and disappear.
My heavy heart disappears.
The farm animals disappear.
The black sea disappears.
The green steam train disappears.
My friends disappear.

Mrs Evans takes my friend Jaya.
Miss Minty takes a girl called Abi.
Mr Kay takes a boy called Zach.
Mrs Glam takes a boy from my school called J.
Miss Skinner takes Maisie and me.
All that remains is a piece of cake and it vanishes.

Eve O'Sullivan (11)
King Henry VIII Preparatory School, Coventry

Destroyer

The water, *whoosh, whoosh!*
Violently like a tiger searching for prey.
Bright beaming shooting stars were the storm lightning,
Thundering, shooting guns blasting in the air.

Slithering through the icy waters,
The Jabberwocky with greenish-yellow scaly skin,
Its teeth as sharp as a diamond,
Agitated by the destructive storm,
It leapt out of the sea and snapped up the dragonhead ship,
Dark, cold and frosty night,

Crush, crush, crush!

The sea was calm as the bright sunny day began,
The Jabberwocky hibernates deep in the aqua sea for the summer
It'll be back.

Mayur Patel (9)
King Henry VIII Preparatory School, Coventry

An Evacuee

Every day I'm missing all my toys for playing inside.
Much to my delight I'm leaving my broken games.
The saddest thing is waving goodbye to my mum and dad.
For this day I will to leave everything as if nothing ever existed.
This is as hard as anything as I say goodbye to my house.
Now it's time to say goodbye.

As I'm on the train, I see farms.
The countryside and the smoke behind me.
I feel sad, lonely on one side, but happy on the other.
I can hear the sound of the train making me sleepy.
Later I hear the train track making a squeaking noise.
I feel that I have no space to myself there.
When I'm chosen I feel I have a strict owner.
I hear the trees going side to side.
I see lots of grass, animals and houses.
I feel pleased that I got chosen unlike in school.
I see the owner looking pleased with me.
The house looked white, large with a yellow roof.

Muhammed Abid (11)
King Henry VIII Preparatory School, Coventry

The Kraken

Sailors sailing the seven seas,
Ship starts rocking, waving violently,
Suddenly, ferocious monster appears.
Monster grasps captain with octopus-like tentacles,
Everyone's hearts thumping like a drum.
Men run frantically grabbing guns and spears,
The monster is gulping people.
Bones heard cracking and desperate screams of sailors,
But the monster is gobbling people.
Jack clambers up the sail, holding on for dear life,
Monster tries to grab him,
Jack fights him like a hero.
The monster has had enough, snaps the ship in two.
Jack dives into the ocean and smells the salty sea.
The boat takes a moment,
Then sinks . . .

Shuva Ranjitkar (9)
King Henry VIII Preparatory School, Coventry

Kraken

In the deep he's lurking,
Waiting to pounce.
Tentacles slither, slide up the boat,
As green as can be.
Suction cups cling on a rough, wooden boat.

Holding on for dear life,
Smell of seawater drifts up noses.
Icy clanking spears freeze shaking hands.
Shouts, bells just heard over splashes,
Grabs men with slimy, scaly tentacles.

Up pops a mouth, covered in blood,
Eating each man, frightened, cold.
Hearts beating so loud you can hear them,
Tentacles grasp, pull down the boat.

Crash!
Then . . .
Silence . . .

Emily Moore (9)
King Henry VIII Preparatory School, Coventry

Dominoes

Here I am
Sitting outside my house.
Well, my rubble pile now.
It seems to be all I can see now
Is my steel bed posts
Poking up from my house's remains.
I am lucky to be alive
Whereas my sister, not so lucky.
I look around the streets of London,
A bombsite.
Standing alone, half a sweet shop.
They were bombed like dominoes,
One after the other,
Knocking over houses,
Wiped out like dominoes.
Streets wiped out like dominoes.

Megan Bestard (10)
King Henry VIII Preparatory School, Coventry

Evacuee Poem

I am an evacuee
Carrying my gas mask and my luggage with me.
People think I'm a country child,
I have an uncommon uniform and a cold coat.
I'm saying goodbye to my parents
And I'm leaving my house and my bed.

I see a farm in the distance with strange looking animals on it.
Choo-choo on the train.
I am excited to see who I stay with.
The train disappears.
My teacher disappears!

Mrs Dublin chose three girls called Georgina, Layla and Esmé.
We all thought she didn't have much room.
I thought my friends and I were chosen, we were.
Mrs Dublin is very kind, she offered us a piece of cake.
I didn't want a piece because I couldn't swallow it,
I felt nervous.

Layla Skinner (11)
King Henry VIII Preparatory School, Coventry

In The Deep

Sea as rough as a rock
Wind like a giant's breath
Loud cracks in the background
Icy cold weather
Thunder loud as a trumpet

Teeth sharp as knives
Body like metal
Slimy like a snail
Big like a giant
Crushing everything in his way

Broken planks everywhere
People dying
Sailors drowning
Shouting and shrieking
Yelling and screaming everywhere.

Dani Haider (10)
King Henry VIII Preparatory School, Coventry

The Evacuees

It's all a blur.
Mum and Dad take me to the station.
There it's a rush of labels, suitcases and kisses.
She cries. He tells her to be strong.
He stands there, his emotions hidden by a military cap.
He lets all but one tear roll down his stone face.
Suddenly the noise of the station is far away.
He smiles. I cry. Then everything comes into focus.
The buzz of the station is back.
Time to get on the train, I board, they watch.
The train starts. I stick a hand out of the window.
She reaches out for it, he stops her.
We begin our journey.
She sobs and cries her heart out.
He stands with a firm salute.
I can't go back, I'm not alone though.
There are others, and we fight with each other.
We are the evacuees.

Felix Marufu (11)
King Henry VIII Preparatory School, Coventry

The Octamunch

The octamunch, the octamunch
Its silver teeth go *cling, clang, crunch.*
Its eight green amazing tentacles
Smashing, bashing, crashing and lashing.
Its pearly smooth transparent skin
Shimmers in the bright rays of the sun.
The icy glow within its florescent eyes
Lets out flames of fury and anger.

The octamunch, the octamunch
His colossal-sized belly growling for lunch.
It slithers majestically through the water
Now it's ready to slaughter.
Its eight tentacles arising from the watery ground
Enveloping and engulfing the ship without a sound.
Then comes crashing down with thunder
Leaving everything asunder.

Davina Mistry (10)
King Henry VIII Preparatory School, Coventry

The Dragafish

The Dragafish,
The Dragafish,
Its eyes are dark and purplish,
Its tail is long and slimyish,
Its blood is cold and yellowish,
Its fangs are sharp and smell like fish,
They're black,
Not blue
And bumpyish.
Its lips are starving hungrily
And slimy,
Sucky,
Blubbery.
The Dragafish,
The Dragafish,
It ate my goldfish called Markish,
When you are tucked up in your bed,
You are about to meet your dread . . .

Niamh Brennan (9)
King Henry VIII Preparatory School, Coventry

The War Is The End

The war is the end
Today we shall make a change
We shall attack with the help of God

The Nazis laughing
At what they did to us
But on our Spitfires we shall drop incendiaries

We burn Berlin
We kill Hitler
We burn the spirits of those Nazis
Then we win.

Our fellow friends
Thank you
For taking down the Nazis
Now we give the Yanks the atomic bomb
To finish off Japan!

Sahib Singh Takhar (10)
King Henry VIII Preparatory School, Coventry

The Storm Monster

The storm is getting closer
They can feel it in the air
Suddenly rain crashes down on them
The sea is as black as coal
Whilst the waves are roaring like lions
They now freeze in the ice cold air.

Suddenly the ship rocks madly
They run to the edge to see what's there
From behind four slimy tentacles appear
Although no sound is heard, fear is all around
The sea monster wildly swings his tentacles around the ship
He plunges one of them through the bottom of the ship
A deadly cracking sound is heard as the ship snaps in two.

Terrified they slip off into the water
They hold their breath hoping to reach surface
Searching madly they try and find something to hold onto
Splash, splash, splash they hear all around.

Joshua Aspinall (9)
King Henry VIII Preparatory School, Coventry

Blue

Blue like the sky on a sunny day,
As blue as the ocean,
Like my brother's bedroom wall.

Blue like a tub of peanuts,
As blue as my mum's eyes,
Like Coventry City Football Club.

Blue like the winter walking on water,
As blue as the navy,
Like a Thomson aeroplane.

Blue like the frost running over the window,
As blue as a card I sent to my dad,
Like my brother's school jumper.

Blue like a sad feeling running through you,
Blue like the dark sky at night.

Charlotte Cawley (10)
King Henry VIII Preparatory School, Coventry

Blitz

Warning siren, siren of death
Tells the city, they are near.
Coming to destroy our homes
Here comes death.

Pitter-patter go the feet
Rushing to a piece of tin,
Rushing to a piece of tin,
That won't keep out a bomb.
Piercing noise of a baby's cry,
Where's Nanny? Don't let her die.

Crawling out of a so-called shelter
Meant to protect, ha! Not true.
The spaghetti-tangled cable torn and askew.
Gingerbread crumpled houses all destroyed and bombed.
Yeah, just like gingerbread except not sweet.
They search for the corpses buried alive,
Let us sing, let us pray, all them taken this very day.

Ethan Latty (10)
King Henry VIII Preparatory School, Coventry

My Giraffe Poem

The giraffe's long neck stretching for food.

His thin legs standing tall
While the giraffe's long neck stretched for food.

A small tail swinging calmly
While his thin legs stood tall
As the giraffe's long neck stretched for food.

A huge tongue pulling off leaves
As a small tail swung calmly
While his thin legs stood tall
As the giraffe's long neck stretched for food.

His patchwork coat blending him into the trees
As a huge tongue pulled off leaves
While his thin legs stood tall
As the giraffe's long neck stretched for food.

Rachel Leigh (8)
King Henry VIII Preparatory School, Coventry

The Craler

Clouds swirling
Wind blowing
All but silent
Lightning is orange not yellow, also jagged
The whole world is black

Fire-red tentacles everywhere
Arm suckers stick to the boat
It feels like the whole world will end
People flying everywhere, it's like a giant screw hit the land
Bang, the boat's in half

The monster goes silent for a minute
Calm
My heart is beating like an elephant jumping up and down
It's freezing, I'm blue, I feel like I'm dying
The wood I'm on breaks
I sink
It's the end.

Christie Neale (9)
King Henry VIII Preparatory School, Coventry

The Monster Comes Alive

It was a dim, dark day as if the sun was not alive,
The laboratory was as cold as an iceberg,
The wind rattled the silky blinds.
Potions were scattered like bird seeds,
In the middle stood an old oak table like a proud dog!

The yellow gooey eye of the monster slowly twitched
Like a trigger of a rifle gun.
Blood dripped from the monster's head
Like splodges of red paint,
Drip, drop, drip.

He had fake hair from a monkey,
Fingernails from dead Sir Francis Drake!
He had small dotty giraffe ears,
He was a total mess!

Hannah Jane Kennedy (11)
King Henry VIII Preparatory School, Coventry

Blitz Poem

Wailing of the death siren deafens my ears.
Everybody rushing, barging people out the way.
Constant screaming and shouting of people.
Annoying sound of the siren rattles in my head.

The howling sound of Nazi bombs.
Spray of bullets fill the jet-black night sky.
Black choking smoke makes me cough viciously.
Rubble scattered over the hard concrete street.
Cascading of incendiaries light up the forest with crimson red fire.
Shudder of the unstable shelter keeps me awake.

Buildings' windows shatter.
Rocks vast as a meteor fill up the street.
Stench of dustbins fill my nostrils.
People huddle together searching for their home.
Tangle of wires like a bowl of spaghetti.
Isolated children sit in devastation outside their demolished houses.
People deserted, abandoned, lost, where is my home?

Callum Durrant (11)
King Henry VIII Preparatory School, Coventry

Sea Poem

The restless, windy sea,
Rough as anything can be smashing against the rocks.
The threatening, thrashing sea scaring the men on the docks.
The swirling whirlpool as strong as you will ever be.
The strong swirling whirlpool, is the last thing you'll ever see.

The rampaging, rushing sea smashing into wooden ships.
The sea always thrashing, making very big dips.
The tsunami taking the sea, destroying sailors.
Their lives lost forever.

Slowly the rough sea starts to calm.
Its hard efforts have come to an end.
The calm, peaceful sea flowing gently.
Its gentle surface like shimmering glass.

George Edwards (9)
King Henry VIII Preparatory School, Coventry

The Evacuees

Took to the station on a misty morning,
Wrapped up warm in our coats.
Saying goodbye to our mothers.
We sobbed and cried,
Hoping it was just a bad dream.
We were pushed onto the train,
Not wanting to leave.
We were the evacuees.

Our fathers, battling at war,
Our mothers, in despair at the station.
Taken to the corner shop to be chosen,
Strong boys and pretty girls were picked first.
I was cold, nervous, desperate for a home,
But, I wasn't chosen.
'Onto the next town,' the warden said,
I was miserable,
I was an evacuee.

Joshua Davenport (11)
King Henry VIII Preparatory School, Coventry

The Kraken

All is quiet, everything normal,
Nobody knows about the kraken underwater, until now . . .
Warning bells ring, men scream out,
Monster lurks beneath the watery sea.
A slithery tentacle rises out of the depths of the water,
Covered in oozing, sucky ulcers, like plungers.
They smash, tear, disintegrate,
Grab innocent men.
Head as large as a galleon,
Death whirling in its eyes as it stares.
Murderous mouth, swallows and gulps,
Teeth sharper than nails.
Panicked men swim away,
But don't escape the kraken.
They drown slowly,
The kraken sinks its pointed jaws into their skin
And swallows.

Thomas Meynell (10)
King Henry VIII Preparatory School, Coventry

Memphis Belle

Memphis Belle
Flying in the air,
Four engines powering their way through,
Brave men killing madmen.

Memphis Belle
Whistling in the dark night sky,
Bombs screaming in the air,
Brave men killing madmen.

Memphis Belle
Gliding in the full moon,
Making cover in the grey clouds,
Brave men killing madmen.

Memphis Belle
Completed the tour of duty,
They were heroes for America,
They were the Memphis Belle.

William Collier (10)
King Henry VIII Preparatory School, Coventry

The Kraken

Wind blows across the sea.
Rumours mutter about the Kraken.
The boat hit something hard.
Slimy tentacles rose up into the air.
Goo dropped,
Bells rang, wood splintered.
Men screaming like little girls.
Knives waving like the wind
Across your face.
Sailors running to save their lives.
Swords ready to fight like they mean it.
Tentacles swooping down to take sailors away,
To their death place.
Tearing tentacles tear the boat apart.
Men falling into cold salty sea.
Screams fade.
The nightmare is over.

Eleni Georgiades (10)
King Henry VIII Preparatory School, Coventry

My Favourite Things!

Roast chicken,
With an ice cream sauce,
Laid in the bath,
Whilst grooming a horse.

Cremated mushrooms,
On a slimy rock,
Served with mayonnaise,
Listening to baroque.

Lamb korma,
With a Malteser garnish,
Watching a film,
Painting my nails with varnish.

Sticky toffee pud,
With a horseradish preserve,
Cracking open walnuts,
In a nature reserve.

Cliona Anson-O'Connell (11)
King Henry VIII Preparatory School, Coventry

The Giant Squid

The clouds get dark and twirling
The rain starts to get heavy and falls rapidly
Lightning zaps quickly
Getting closer and closer
The air freezing cold as ice
Getting colder and colder
Suddenly
Tentacles slither up the ship
Striking quickly, wrapping around people
Squishing them hardly
Round mouth, sharp teeth eating people
Munch, munch
Crunch, crunch
Slowly it goes back into the water
People shouting,
'Help us, help us!'
Glug, glug, glug!

James Maclean (10)
King Henry VIII Preparatory School, Coventry

The Kraken

As the innocent pirates turn their bony backs
A ferocious monster lurks about the seven seas,
Tentacles as glutinous as suction cups
Swipe defenceless pirates to bay.

Helpless pirates squabble and shout,
But the cannibalistic monster has no sympathy,
With a mouth as big as an elephant
It just tears them up in its fetid mouth.

The venomous kraken descends to the pungent seas after its tiring hunt
And the annihilated ship is left alone,
Bubbles tower,
The kraken descends
And
        everything
                goes
                        quiet . . .

Kelechi Apakama (9)
King Henry VIII Preparatory School, Coventry

Evacuee Poem

Goodbye old town, goodbye Mum and Dad,
Goodbye factories, I'll never see you again,
Goodbye this little school, friend and teachers too,
Goodbye this little park, one day I'll see you soon,
Goodbye greengrocers, sorry I nicked your fruit,
Goodbye this small house, I hope you don't get bombed.

I'm on the train, I'm feeling sad and lonely,
I'm on the train, my heart's pumping quickly,
I'm on the train, I'm seeing the grey smoke,
I'm on the train, *clicky, clacky, clicky, clacky, click,*
I'm on the train and tears are bursting out slowly.

The lady's really strict, she thinks I'm poor,
The lady's really strict, she gives me cat food,
The lady's really strict, all she does is sing,
The lady's really strict, you'd better not go in her room,
The lady's really strict, I absolutely hate her.

Pavinder Suprai (11)
King Henry VIII Preparatory School, Coventry

The Elegant Zebra With Unique Stripes

Hooves clicking and clapping quickly.

Small ears whipping around sensitively
As the hooves were clicking and clapping quickly.

Legs stirring steeply down the hill
While the small ears started whipping around sensitively
As the hooves were clicking and clapping quickly.

Tail beautifully wagging gently
As the legs were stirring steeply down the hill,
While the small ears started whipping around sensitively,
As the hooves were clicking and clapping quickly.

Mouth chewing the grass slowly
As the tail beautifully wagged gently,
As the legs were stirring steeply down the hill
While the small ears started whipping around sensitively,
As the hooves were clicking and clapping quickly.

Jason Adams (8)
King Henry VIII Preparatory School, Coventry

Lion Poem

The powerful golden lion instantly leapt on.

Teeth as sharp as knives dug deeply into the victim
That the powerful golden lion instantly leapt on.

Strong limbs sprinting energetically to its target,
Teeth as sharp as knives dug deeply into the victim
That the powerful golden lion instantly leapt on.

Razor claws grabbed the powerless fiercely,
Strong limbs sprinting energetically to its target,
Teeth as sharp as knives dug deeply into the victim
That the powerful golden lion instantly leapt on.

Eyes spying continuously like a hawk on its prey,
Razor claws grabbed the powerless fiercely,
Strong limbs sprinting energetically to its target,
Teeth as sharp as knives dug deeply into the victim
That the powerful golden lion instantly leapt on.

Sulayman Janjua (8)
King Henry VIII Preparatory School, Coventry

Lion Poem

The powerful lion pouncing through the savannah.

Shoulders moving up and down, slinking through the grass,
On a powerful lion pounding through the savannah.

Golden mane swishing in the wind
With shoulders moving up and down, slinking through the grass
On the powerful lion pouncing through the savannah.

Long tail moving to and fro
With a golden mane swishing in the wind
With shoulders moving up and down, slinking through the grass
On the powerful lion pounding through the savannah.

Massive feet stomping through the grass
And a long tail moving to and fro
With a golden mane swishing in the wind
With shoulders moving up and down, slinking through the grass
On the powerful lion pounding through the savannah.

Georgia Griffin (8)
King Henry VIII Preparatory School, Coventry

Lion

The lion's golden eyes glittering in the sun.

His shaggy mane like a wreath around his neck,
The lion's golden eyes glittering in the sun.

Upright ears listening for the delicious prey,
His shaggy mane like a wreath around his neck,
The lion's golden eyes glittering in the sun.

Sharp teeth tearing viciously,
Upright ears listening for the delicious prey,
His shaggy mane like a wreath around his neck,
The lion's golden eyes glittering in the sun.

Strong tail swishing violently,
Sharp teeth tearing viciously,
Upright ears listening for the delicious prey,
His shaggy mane like a wreath around his neck,
The lion's golden eyes glittering in the sun.

Emily Nicholls (9)
King Henry VIII Preparatory School, Coventry

The Lion

The magnificent lion lying peacefully in the shade.

Golden mane glistening in the brightness of the yellow sun
While the magnificent lion lying peacefully in the shade.

Tail with a tassel at the tip swaying in the warm air
As the golden mane glistens in the brightness of the yellow sun
While the magnificent lion lying peacefully in the shade.

Long sharp fangs devouring the scrumptious meat
With tail with a tassel at the tip swaying in the warm air
As the golden mane glistens in the brightness of the yellow sun
While the magnificent lion lying peacefully in the shade.

With claws of steel the hunting lion kills his prey swiftly
With long sharp fang devouring the scrumptious meat
With tail with a tassel at the tip swaying in the warm air
As the golden mane glistens in the brightness of the yellow sun
While the magnificent lion lying peacefully in the shade.

Jasmine Close (9)
King Henry VIII Preparatory School, Coventry

Blitz Poem

The familiar howl of the air raid siren.
Feared by all the people rampaging to their shelters.
Crying children sprinting away from the deafening screech.
Hundreds waiting for the all-clear, to them the best sound.

The whirring sound of the German bomber making everyone silent.
The whistling sound of a bomb causing chaos in an instant.
Smoke creeping through the entrance making everyone choke.
Rubble falling in, making people reluctant to see the devastation.

Bodies of innocent people placed around battered shelters.
Tears coming out of millions of eyes, horror masking their faces.
Flames reaching as far as the eye could see from the skeletons of fragile looking buildings.
It happened but not again.

Karan Jutti (11)
King Henry VIII Preparatory School, Coventry

What Can It Be?

Swirling grey clouds in the sky,
Air as cold as ice.

The dark black sea filled with dead bodies,
The vast ship swaying rapidly from side to side.

Death is in the air!
Tentacles slithering up the sides of the vast ship,
Crash!

A massive arm smashes the ship into pieces,
All I hear is screaming, 'Help, help!''

All I see is darkness . . .
After the storm has ended I go *glug, glug, glug*.

Reanne Diane Smith (9)
King Henry VIII Preparatory School, Coventry

The Kraken

As the waves crash,
The wind roars like a lion,
And the black cloud rises,
It spreads its darkness all around.

Then a *creak!*
Then chaos as tentacles smash
And the boat cracks.
Men go flying as tentacles throw them through the air.

Then all is quiet as boats sink deep in the water,
And no one is left surviving
As the water calms.

Luke Manning (9)
King Henry VIII Preparatory School, Coventry

The Deep, Deep Squid

A bear of swirling cloud like a twister
Howling wind of the deadly storm
Sailors scrambling and wriggling

Bright electric tentacles zap the sea in two seconds
The sailors shout, 'Help, help, help!'
The giant squid reaches upon the boat as it cracks into two pieces
His teeth glow as sharp as knives
Stomp, stomp, stomp!

They smell fear in the air
They try to get ashore, but they're slow
Glug, glug, glug!

Emily Smith (9)
King Henry VIII Preparatory School, Coventry

Stormy Sea Poem

Stormy crashing waves slapping angrily
Thin freezing water twirling crazily
Clipping crabs moving lightly
Stinging white foam bubbling quickly
Hard, heavy, jagged rocks lurking silently
Wet, crumbling sand moving with the water slowly.

Aasim Ahmed (8)
King Henry VIII Preparatory School, Coventry

Monster Poem

Gigantic beast yawns horribly.
Pointy fangs leering violently.
Glowing eyes as red as blood.
Rotten gums show horribly.
Shrunken skin as rough as a rock.

Gurjeevan Aujla (9)
King Henry VIII Preparatory School, Coventry

Being An Evacuee

I would be heartbroken leaving my mum,
I would have left all my games behind,
Would have been sad leaving my room, houses and shops,
I would have been scared and worried about leaving,
Would be sad and tired,
Bye Mum and Dad, I'll miss you.

I'm on the clicky-clacky train, my heart empty with no love inside it,
Looking outside the window seeing cows, horses and sheep,
I'm tired with nothing to sleep on,
I'm filled with hunger and thirst,
No friends to play with,
I'm bored, in one place all the time.

Just stepped out seeing people, houses and shops,
Been taken to the village hall,
Someone is going to pick us,
The lady is so strict, the lady is shouting at us all the time,
The lady gives me one sausage,
The lady sings which is so annoying.

Nikhil Trivedi (10)
King Henry VIII Preparatory School, Coventry

Penguins

P enguins lay eggs.
E ggs are held in the brood pouch.
N ice penguins.
G o to hunt for food.
U nderwater they swim.
I n the brood pouch are eggs.
N aughty emperor penguins.
S uper penguins.

Oliver Walker (5)
Ravensmead Primary School, Bignall End

Penguins

P addle
E gg
N ice
G racious
U gly
I ce
N ails
S ea.

Amelia Mayer (5)
Ravensmead Primary School, Bignall End

Penguins

P enguin
E nchanted
N ice
G reedy
U seful
I ce
N ice
S wim.

Faith Bell (5)
Ravensmead Primary School, Bignall End

Penguins

P enguins
E nchanted
N ice
G ood
U nderwater
I ce
N ice
S uper penguins.

Dominic Smith (5)
Ravensmead Primary School, Bignall End

Penguin

P enguins have black and white feathers.
E mperor penguins are the rulers.
N ails help the penguins to grip on the ice.
G reat at swimming but they can't fly.
U nder the ice to catch some fish.
I mpossble to fly for a penguin.
N aughty.

Rebecca Walley (7)
Ravensmead Primary School, Bignall End

Penguin

P enguins eat squid and fish
E ggs hatch when the female goes to get food
N eeds food
G o a long way to get some food
U nusual penguins are called Macaroni
I n Antarctica penguins live
N o penguins can fly.

Thomas Mainwaring (6)
Ravensmead Primary School, Bignall End

Penguin

P enguins have black back to camouflage themselves.
E mperor penguins lay their eggs in spring.
N asty predators like to eat their chicks.
G ood divers.
U nderwater.
I n the water they look for food.
N ame giving to the area around the North Pole.

Jessica Mollart-Price (6)
Ravensmead Primary School, Bignall End

My Pet

My Pet
  C at is cute
  A nd soft
  T iptoes about.

Pippa Bradeley (4)
Ravenemead Primary School, Bignall End

Grendel Poem

Grendel, your slimy, slender muscular body races like a cheetah,
Its dark spots make people dizzy.

Grendel, your red and green blood rolling eyes follow people wherever they go,
They never blink just waiting for the right move to . . .

Grendel, your vampire fangs are like a person eating chicken, they go up and down.
They snap and crunch, rip off human heads and skin.

Grendel, your grabbing sharp claws, they grab people one by one.

Grendel, your growling, deep roaring voice makes the birds fly away.

Grendel, your ways scared people out of town.

Why are you like this?

Awase Iyol (10)
St Patrick's Catholic Primary School, Walsall

Grendel

Grendel, your slimy, muscular body is so strong it could demolish a house.
Grendel, your venomous eyes stare at your prey. They are dragon eyes.
Grendel, your beastly teeth are as sharp as a razor. They gnaw bones.
Grendel, your huge claws are like daggers. They rip people.
Grendel, your bellowing voice growls like a wolf. You scare people from a mile away.
Grendel, your evil ways made people horrified of you.
Will you change your ways?

Sebastian Kalicun (9)
St Patrick's Catholic Primary School, Walsall

Grendel

Grendel, your muscular body races faster than a cheetah
But is never slower than a tortoise.

Never happy, never sad, but always mad.
Grendel, your red rolling poisonous eyes stare fiercely at the poor innocent people.

Grendel, your disgusting, crunching, yellow, dirty, razor-sharp teeth are as sharp as a knife.
Snaps worse than an alligator's teeth.

Your keen sword claws can tear humans apart,
Now I know why people get scared!
Your loud, shouting, deafening ears deeper than thunder scares your roaring, screaming, shrieking, yelling voice, that's all I hear every night!

Ayanna Kamose (10)
St Patrick's Catholic Primary School, Walsall

Grendel

Grendel, your muscular hairy body is like a lion going to catch his furry mouse for dinner.

Grendel, your red rolling eyes are like evil devil eyes trying to fiercely scare people away.

Grendel, your razor-sharp teeth are like knives, they snap and crunch human bones.

Grendel, your mighty heavy claws are like a crocodile's teeth waiting for its prey.

Grendel, your threatening echoing voice sounds like someone is screaming for help and lost their voice.

Evie Mansell (10)
St Patrick's Catholic Primary School, Walsall

Grendel Poem

Grendel, your scaly body is as scaly as a scaly snake
And as hairy as a hairy hyena.

Grendel, your eyes are as red as red revolting lava
And as round as a sphere.

Grendel, your teeth are as sharp as a blade
And as black as coal.

Grendel, your claws crunch and snap people's bones.

Grendel, your voice is like a volcano exploding.

Grendel you are so mean and evil.

Joao Cariata (10)
St Patrick's Catholic Primary School, Walsall

Grendel!

Grendel, your slimy body speeds like a leopard.
Grendel, your blood-red rolling eyes stare like a devil.
Grendel, your sharp yellow rotten teeth are like claws.
They crunch and shred people's bones.
Grendel, your sharp steely claws are like knives.
They scratch and rip people to pieces.
Grendel, your low pitch voice is like thunder at night.
It roars like a werewolf.
Grendel, you scare people at night when they are sleeping.
Grendel, everyone is terrified of you,
They won't even step out the house if they know you are around.

Libby Taylor (9)
St Patrick's Catholic Primary School, Walsall

Grendel

Grendel, your hairy body racing like a leopard.
Grendel, your slimy rotten teeth eat like a blade hitting a tree.
Grendel, your red rolling eyes scare like a devil.
Grendel, your claws are as sharp as a blade.
Grendel, your voice is deep howling like a fox.
Grendel, your feelings make other people scared of you.

Callum Marshall (9)
St Patrick's Catholic Primary School, Walsall

Grendel

Grendel, your sticky and slippery slug body races like a cheetah.
Grendel, your red angry eyes filled with fury.
Your eyes staring at people.
Grendel, your yellow rotten teeth are rusty and smelly.
They are crunching the human bones.
Grendel, your spiky hard claws are like knives.
Your claws scratching the walls.
Grendel, your loud howling voice scaring people away.
Your voice howling like a wolf.
Grendel, people are scared of you.

Sonia Chopra (9)
St Patrick's Catholic Primary School, Walsall

Grendel

Grendel, your sticky hairy body is as fast as a cheetah
That goes sneaking down the street to catch your prey.
Grendel, your red rolling eyes are like pin pricks,
Glaring at your enemies in your town.
Grendel, your mighty strong teeth are like blades opening and closing
When you catch your prey.
Grendel, your razor-sharp claws are as black as coal.
Your claws can rip anyone apart.
Grendel, your deeply loud voice growls like a lion that roars at a baby.
Do you think you are a match for Grendel?

Levi Mason (10)
St Patrick's Catholic Primary School, Walsall

Grendel

Grendel, your slimy body is as sticky as a snail's body!
Grendel, your red, venomous eyes which are filled with fury pierce fiercely like darts!
Grendel, your jagged, beastly teeth are like sharp knives!
Grendel, your huge black claws, which tear humans to pieces, are as black as coal!
Grendel, your bellowing voice growls as loud as a volcano about to erupt!
Grendel, your violent ways make people horrified of you!

Nikisha Ward (10)
St Patrick's Catholic Primary School, Walsall

Grendel

Grendel, your muscular hairy body races like a cheetah!
Grendel, your blood rolling eyes stare fiercely at the villagers like a devil.
Grendel, your black razor teeth can shred up anything.
Grendel, your mighty black claws are heavy as a ton for shredding up anything.
Grendel, your sharp growling voice threatens the villagers with fright.
Grendel, you make the villagers feel terrified and petrified of you.
Grendel, you're mighty and scary and petrifying.

Courtney Ryan (10)
St Patrick's Catholic Primary School, Walsall

Grendel

Grendel, your hairy body is slithering like a fish
And evil heart is as hard as stone.
Grendel, your eyes are like red rolling crocodile eyes.
Grendel, your sharp scratching claws.
Grendel, your big rotten yellow teeth.
Grendel, your voice is dark and rough.
Grendel, your petrifying slimy body makes people scared.

Todd Edmunds (9)
St Patrick's Catholic Primary School, Walsall

Grendel

Grendel, your filthy, furry body rambles like a dog.
Grendel, your ruby red eyes are sharp as flames.
Grendel, your golden yellow teeth tear like razors.
Grendel, your hammer hand is like a thousand boulders.
Grendel, your deep, dark voice roars like a lion.
Grendel, your fiendish ways make people petrified of you!

Becki Lang (10)
St Patrick's Catholic Primary School, Walsall

You!

You!
Your fangs are as sharp as scissors.
You!
Your legs are good at pouncing like springs.
You!
Your spine is like bumps in the road.
You!
You're a good prowler like a silent night jaguar.

Sophie Fitzpatrick (11)
Springfield House Special School, Knowle

You!

You!
Your coat is like a jungle.
You!
Your legs are fast as a car.
You!
Your eyes are like a thin knife.
You!
Your tail is like a snake.

Thomas Harvey (10)
Springfield House Special School, Knowle

The Moon

The moon is a black wolf
That creeps out
From a dark cave
Walking alone
Crying in the night.

Peter Haden (10)
Springfield House Special School, Knowle

Thunder And Lightning

Thunder is so strong,
That we can play ping-pong,
When we go past,
It gets fast.

Thunder gets scary,
We get hairy,
When thunder strikes
Everyone says, 'Yikes.'

People get scared,
Everyone gets spared,
When thunders talk
They start to stalk.

It cuts through people like a knife,
A man just lost his wife.

It's a mountain,
People like to pound the king,
It's an earthquake,
Trying to break a cake.

Lightning is so fast,
It's like a dark blast,
When lightning says hello,
What would you say back?

Qasim Ali (10)
Ward End Primary School, Birmingham

Thunder

Thunder is like a big tornado,
Rushing through the atmosphere,
Feels like a shocking fear.

Flaming through the empty streets,
Terrorising everything in its path,
If it bites you, it will kill you.

It is a running cheetah,
Racing through the streets.
Will you ever get hit by thunder?

Tahir Mohammed (9)
Ward End Primary School, Birmingham

Bored

I'm so bored,
Sitting on the settee.
I'm so bored,
Can't you see?

I'm so bored,
I want to watch TV.
But I have to revise for a grammar test,
So I can get a Nintendo Wii.

I want to go to my friend's house,
But I'm not allowed.
My life's so boring
And so I don't feel proud.

I'm so bored,
Sitting on the settee.
I'm so bored,
Can't you see?
So bored, so bored.
Help!

Aisha Amjad (10)
Ward End Primary School, Birmingham

Driving Me Mad

My brother's crying, wailing,
My sister's trying,
It's driving me mad,
Quieten them down.

My father's exercising (too much),
My mother's frying,
Just stop them!
They are driving me mad!

Baby's crying, (too loud),
Aunty's moaning,
Make them quiet,
They're driving me mad.

Sara Said (10)
Ward End Primary School, Birmingham

Thunder

Thunder is an electric shock,
A tornado going round, round, round,
Is like sizzling lights,
It's an angry man who has never got peace,
As quick as a flash like lightning,
Like a volcano erupting,
An earthquake which is going *bang,*
Do you like thunder?

Tahreem Hussain (9)
Ward End Primary School, Birmingham

Maddie's Workshop

Featured Author:

Maddie Stewart

Maddie is a children's writer, poet and author who currently lives in Coney Island, Northern Ireland.

Maddie has 5 published children's books, 'Cinders', 'Hal's Sleepover', 'Bertie Rooster', 'Peg' and 'Clever Daddy'. Maddie uses her own unpublished work to provide entertaining, interactive poems and rhyming stories for use in her workshops with children when she visits schools, libraries, arts centres and book festivals. Favourites are 'Silly Billy, Auntie Millie' and 'I'm a Cool, Cool Kid'. Maddie works throughout Ireland from her home in County Down. She is also happy to work from a variety of bases in England. She has friends and family, with whom she regularly stays, in Leicester, Bedford, London and Ashford (Kent). Maddie's workshops are aimed at 5-11-year-olds. Check out Maddie's website for all her latest news and free poetry resources **www.maddiestewart.com**.

Read on to pick up some fab writing tips!

Nonsense Workshop

If you find silliness fun,
you will love nonsense poems.
Nonsense poems might describe silly things,
or people, or situations,
or, any combination of the three.

For example:

When I got out of bed today,
both my arms had run away.
I sent my feet to fetch them back.
When they came back, toe in hand
I realised what they had planned.
They'd made the breakfast I love most,
buttered spider's eggs on toast.

**One way to find out if you enjoy nonsense poems
is to start with familiar nursery rhymes.
Ask your teacher to read them out,
putting in the names of some children in your class.**

Like this: Troy and Jill went up the hill
to fetch a pail of water.
Troy fell down
and broke his crown
and Jill came tumbling after.

If anyone is upset at the idea of using their name, then don't use it.

Did you find this fun?

Maddie's Workshop

**Now try changing a nursery rhyme.
Keep the rhythm and the rhyme style, but invent a silly situation.**

Like this: Hickory Dickory Dare
a pig flew up in the air.
The clouds above
gave him a shove
Hickory Dickory Dare.

Or this: Little Miss Mabel
sat at her table
eating a strawberry pie
but a big, hairy beast
stole her strawberry feast
and made poor little Mabel cry.

How does your rhyme sound if you put your own name in it?

Another idea for nonsense poems is to pretend letters are people and have them do silly things.

For example:
Mrs A	Mrs B	Mrs C
Lost her way	Dropped a pea	Ate a tree

**To make your own 'Silly People Poem', think of a word to use.
To show you an example, I will choose the word 'silly'.
Write your word vertically down the left hand side of your page.
Then write down some words which rhyme
with the sound of each letter.**

S mess, dress, Bess, chess, cress
I eye, bye, sky, guy, pie, sky
L sell, bell, shell, tell, swell, well
L " " " " " " (" means the same as written above)
Y (the same words as those rhyming with I)

Use your rhyming word lists to help you make up your poem.

Mrs S made a mess
Mrs I ate a pie
Mrs L rang a bell
Mrs L broke a shell
Mrs Y said 'Bye-bye.'

**You might even make a 'Silly Alphabet' by using
all the letters of the alphabet.**

**It is hard to find rhyming words for all the letters.
H, X and W are letters which are hard to match with rhyming words.
I'll give you some I've thought of:**

H - cage, stage, wage (close but not perfect)
X - flex, specs, complex, Middlesex
W - trouble you, chicken coop, bubble zoo

**However, with nonsense poems, you can use nonsense words.
You can make up your own words.**

**To start making up nonsense words you could
try mixing dictionary words together.
Let's make up some nonsense animals.**

Make two lists of animals. (You can include birds and fish as well.)

Your lists can be as long as you like. These are lists I made:

elephant	kangaroo
tiger	penguin
lizard	octopus
monkey	chicken

**Now use the start of an animal on one list and substitute
it for the start of an animal from your other list.**

I might use the start of oct/opus ... oct and substitute it for the end of l/izard
to give me a new nonsense animal ... an octizard.
I might swap the start of monk/ey ... monk with the end of kang/aroo
To give me another new nonsense animal ... a monkaroo.

What might a monkaroo look like? What might it eat?

**You could try mixing some food words in the same way,
to make up nonsense foods.**

cabbage	potatoes
lettuce	parsley
bacon	crisps

**Cribbage, bacley, and lettatoes are some nonsense foods
made up from my lists.**

Let's see if I can make a nonsense poem about my monkaroo.

Maddie's Workshop

> My monkaroo loves bacley.
> He'll eat lettatoes too
> But his favourite food is cribbage
> Especially if it's blue.

Would you like to try and make up your own nonsense poem?

**Nonsense words don't have to be a combination of dictionary words.
They can be completely 'made up'.
You can use nonsense words to write nonsense sonnets,
or list poems or any type of poem you like.**

Here is a poem full of nonsense words:

> I melly micked a turdle
> and flecked a pendril's tum.
> I plotineyed a shugat
> and dracked a pipin's plum.

Ask your teacher to read it putting in some children's names instead of the first I, and he or she instead of the second I.

Did that sound funny?

You might think that nonsense poems are just silly and not for the serious poet. However poets tend to love language. Making up your own words is a natural part of enjoying words and sounds and how they fit together. Many poets love the freedom nonsense poems give them. Lots and lots of very famous poets have written nonsense poems. I'll name some: **Edward Lear**, **Roger McGough**, **Lewis Carroll**, **Jack Prelutsky** and **Nick Toczek**. Can you or your teacher think of any more? For help with a class nonsense poem or to find more nonsense nursery rhymes look on my website, **www.maddiestewart.com**. Have fun! Maddie Stewart.

Poetry Techniques

Here is a selection of poetry techniques with examples

Metaphors & Similes

A *metaphor* is when you describe your subject *as* something else, for example:
'Winter is a cruel master leaving the servants in a bleak wilderness'
whereas a *simile* describes your subject *like* something else i.e.
'His blue eyes are like ice-cold puddles' or 'The flames flickered like eyelashes'.

Personification

This is to simply give a personality to something that is not human, for example 'Fear spreads her uneasiness around' or 'Summer casts down her warm sunrays'.

Imagery

To use words to create mental pictures of what you are trying to convey, your poem should awaken the senses and make the reader feel like they are in that poetic scene …
'The sky was streaked with pink and red as shadows cast across the once-golden sand'.
'The sea gently lapped the shore as the palm trees rustled softly in the evening breeze'.

Assonance & Alliteration

Alliteration uses a repeated constant sound and this effect can be quite striking:
'Smash, slippery snake slithered sideways'.
Assonance repeats a significant vowel or vowel sound to create an impact:
'The pool looked cool'.

Poetry Techniques

Repetition

By repeating a significant word the echo effect can be a very powerful way of enhancing an emotion or point your poem is putting across.
'The blows rained down, down,
Never ceasing,
Never caring
About the pain,
The pain'.

Onomatopoeia

This simply means you use words that sound like the noise you are describing, for example 'The rain *pattered* on the window' or 'The tin can *clattered* up the alley'.

Rhythm & Metre

The *rhythm* of a poem means 'the beat', the sense of movement you create. The placing of punctuation and the use of syllables affect the *rhythm* of the poem. If your intention is to have your poem read slowly, use double, triple or larger syllables and punctuate more often, where as if you want to have a fast-paced read use single syllables, less punctuation and shorter sentences.
If you have a regular rhythm throughout your poem this is known as *metre*.

Enjambment

This means you don't use punctuation at the end of your line, you simply let the line flow on to the next one. It is commonly used and is a good word to drop into your homework!

Tone & Lyric

The poet's intention is expressed through their *tone*. You may feel happiness, anger, confusion, loathing or admiration for your poetic subject. Are you criticising or praising? How you feel about your topic will affect your choice of words and therefore your *tone*. For example 'I *loved* her', 'I *cared* for her', 'I *liked* her'.
If you write the poem from a personal view or experience this is referred to as a *lyrical* poem. A good example of a lyrical poem is Seamus Heaney's 'Mid-term Break' or any sonnet!

All About Shakespeare

Try this fun quiz with your family, friends or even in class!

1. Where was Shakespeare born?

....

2. Mercutio is a character in which Shakepeare play?

....

3. Which monarch was said to be 'quite a fan' of his work?

....

4. How old was he when he married?

....

5. What is the name of the last and 'only original' play he wrote?

....

6. What are the names of King Lear's three daughters?

....

7. Who is Anne Hathaway?

....

All About Shakespeare

8. Which city is the play 'Othello' set in?

....

9. Can you name 2 of Shakespeare's 17 comedies?

....

10. 'This day is call'd the feast of Crispian: He that outlives this day, and comes safe home, Will stand a tip-toe when this day is nam'd, and rouse him at the name of Crispian' is a quote from which play?

....

11. Leonardo DiCaprio played Romeo in the modern day film version of Romeo and Juliet. Who played Juliet in the movie?

....

12. Three witches famously appear in which play?

....

13. Which famous Shakespearean character is Eric in the image to the left?

....

14. What was Shakespeare's favourite poetic form?

....

Answers are printed on the last page of the book, good luck!

If you would rather try the quiz online,
you can do so at www.youngwriters.co.uk.

Poetry Activity

Word Soup

**To help you write a poem, or even a story,
on any theme, you should create word soup!**

If you have a theme or subject for your poem, base your word soup on it.
If not, don't worry, the word soup will help you find a theme.

To start your word soup you need ingredients:

- Nouns (names of people, places, objects, feelings, i.e. Mum, Paris, house, anger)
- Colours
- Verbs ('doing words', i.e. kicking, laughing, running, falling, smiling)
- Adjectives (words that describe nouns, i.e. tall, hairy, hollow, smelly, angelic)

We suggest at least 5 of each from the above list, this will make sure your word soup has plenty of choice. Now, if you have already been given a theme or title for your poem, base your ingredients on this. If you have no idea what to write about, write down whatever you like, or ask a teacher or family member to give you a theme to write about.

Poetry Activity

Making Word Soup

Next, you'll need a sheet of paper.
Cut it into at least 20 pieces. Make sure the pieces are big enough to write your ingredients on, one ingredient on each piece of paper.
Write your ingredients on the pieces of paper.
Shuffle the pieces of paper and put them all in a box or bowl
- something you can pick the paper out of without looking at the words.
Pick out 5 words to start and use them to write your poem!

Example:

Our theme is winter. Our ingredients are:
- Nouns: snowflake, Santa, hat, Christmas, snowman.
- Colours: blue, white, green, orange, red.
- Verbs: ice-skating, playing, laughing, smiling, wrapping.
- Adjectives: cold, tall, fast, crunchy, sparkly.

**Our word soup gave us these 5 words:
snowman, red, cold, hat, fast and our poem goes like this:**

It's a *cold* winter's day,
My nose and cheeks are *red*
As I'm outside, building my *snowman*,
I add a *hat* and a carrot nose to finish,
I hope he doesn't melt too *fast*!

**Tip: add more ingredients to your word soup
and see how many different poems you can write!**

**Tip: if you're finding it hard to write a poem with
the words you've picked, swap a word with another one!**

**Tip: try adding poem styles and techniques,
such as assonance or haiku to your soup for an added challenge!**

Young Writers Information

We hope you have enjoyed reading this book - and that you will continue to enjoy it in the coming years.

If you like reading and writing poetry drop us a line, or give us a call, and we'll send you a free information pack.

Alternatively, if you would like to order further copies of this book or any of our other titles, then please give us a call or log onto our website at www.youngwriters.co.uk.

Young Writers Information
Remus House
Coltsfoot Drive
Peterborough
PE2 9BF
Tel: (01733) 890066
Fax: (01733) 313524

Email: info@youngwriters.co.uk

Shakespeare Quiz Answers

1. Stratford-upon-Avon **2.** Romeo and Juliet **3.** James I **4.** 18 **5.** The Tempest **6.** Regan, Cordelia and Goneril **7.** His wife **8.** Venice **9.** All's Well That Ends Well, As You Like It, The Comedy of Errors, Cymbeline, Love's Labour's Lost, Measure for Measure, The Merchant of Venice, The Merry Wives of Windsor, A Midsummer Night's Dream, Much Ado About Nothing, Pericles - Prince of Tyre, The Taming of the Shrew, The Tempest, Twelfth Night, The Two Gentlemen of Verona, Troilus & Cressida, The Winter's Tale **10.** Henry V **11.** Claire Danes **12.** Macbeth **13.** Hamlet **14.** Sonnet